Parisian Frilled Canaries – Variegated and Self Green

Plate 26

Red Canary – Flighted Red Orange

CANARY STANDARDS
IN
COLOUR

OTHER TITLES AVAILABLE

Cult of the Budgerigar
W. Watmough revised by Cyril Rogers

The Budgerigar Book
E. Howson

The Lizard Canary and other Rare Breeds
G.T. Dodwell

Humming Birds
A.J. Mobbs

The Yorkshire Canary
E. Howson

Shackleton's Yorkshire Canary
Revised by W.E. Brooks

CANARY STANDARDS IN COLOUR

An Exhibitor's Guide
to the Canary Fancy

By

G.T. DODWELL

Illustrated by JOHN W. HILLS

NIMROD PRESS LTD
PO Box 1
Liss
Hants, GU33 7PR
England

ISBN 1-85259-004-1 (Standard Edition)
ISBN 1-85259-009-2 (Special Edition)

Printed & bound by
R J Acford Chichester
Sussex

Published by
NIMROD PRESS LTD
PO Box 1
Liss, Hants, UK

CONTENTS

BLACK AND WHITE ILLUSTRATIONS

LIST OF COLOUR PLATES

Plate

PREFACE

During the past one hundred years many books on the subject of canaries have been published. They have ranged from small, cheap editions with fairly limited basic information, through monographs for the specialist dealing with one breed of canary only, to large and detailed volumes that covered every aspect of the hobby.

Most have included details of canary culture that may be regarded as essential for the beginner, such as housing, feeding, general management, breeding, moulting and exhibiting. The larger works usually also dealt with each breed at reasonable length and often included the official standards as approved by the various specialist societies extant at the time.

No book, however, exists within the canary fancy comparable with the *British Poultry Standards* or *Fancy Pigeon Standards* which serve the enthusiasts in those particular hobbies by bringing together under one cover all of the official breed standards. It is to fill this gap that the present work has been compiled and my thanks are due to the many specialist societies for permission to include their standards in order to make this a complete and accurate book of reference.

Most of the old books of the larger kind, published during Victorian and Edwardian times, were lavishly illustrated with colour plates, half-tone plates and black and white line drawings. The skill of the artists employed was somewhat variable but the best of them were really superb in their depiction of the various breeds according to the ideals of their time. Most of them, however, are now outdated as standards have improved and so cannot be used again.

In a modern work it might be imagined that, with the present advanced techniques in bird photography, the problem of illustrations would be easily solved; this, however, has not turned out to be the case, especially for the "type" breeds where perfection of form is essential. Canaries are such volatile creatures and cannot be expected to stand motionless while their portraits are taken as, for example dogs or horses might be. Even a bird that is apparently keeping quite still is full of tiny movements almost imperceptible to the naked eye. These are readily recorded by the camera and, as a result, it is impossible to photograph any canary showing off *all* of its good points at one and the same time — it would need a composite of dozens of photographs to come anywhere near it!

Thus, for the present volume, we have turned once again to the art of canary portraiture which has had its respected exponents of the past ranging from J.W. Ludlow, more than a century ago, through A.F. Lydon and Harry Norman to R.A. Vowles, perhaps the last of the "greats", who died some twenty years ago. In the present artist, John W. Hills, we have found a very worthy successor to these illustrious names and I am certain that his paintings will give endless satisfaction and pleasure to the many thousands of fanciers, not only in Great Britain, but all over the world wherever canaries are kept.

High Wycombe   G.T.D.

Chapter 1

STANDARDS AND SPECIALIST SOCIETIES

DEVELOPMENTS

No written records of the earliest standards have survived, if indeed they ever existed. Our oldest breeds of canary date back to the latter part of the eighteenth century, or the early years of the nineteenth, and were essentially local in their origins. Any standards that came into existence would have been arrived at purely by means of visual and verbal appraisal, mutually agreed upon by the groups of fanciers who were involved in their foundation. In this manner, in course of time, from among the generality of nondescript domestic canaries, distinctly recognisable breeds began to emerge some of which, like the Lizard, have survived virtually unchanged down to the present day. Others, though still existing in name, have undergone considerable change since the inception of the breed so that, for example, the Norwich canary of today is quite unlike its forbears of a century and half ago.

In the latter part of the nineteenth century the gradual improvement in general education resulted in the publication of the earliest handbooks dealing with the canary fancy, some of them being fairly modest efforts and others extremely comprehensive volumes on the subject, often being lavishly illustrated. Among the latter, some have become recognised as classics of their kind and copies of them in good condition command high prices in the antiquarian book market of today.

It was in these early handbooks of a century ago that written standards of the various breeds of canary first appeared, mostly being of the author's own devising. They may possibly have been arrived at after consultation with other experts in each particular field, although no indication of this is given, and it is more than likely that the writer himself, often a leading judge and acknowledged authority of his period, was the sole initiator of the standard as printed, especially as they varied from book to book.

This is made quite clear, for instance, by referring to W.A. Blakston, author of the canary section in Cassell's *Book of Canaries and Cage Birds* (written circa 1878) who, at the end of his chapters on Norwich canaries, wrote:

> *"We append a series of Scales in which we have endeavoured to express the approximate and relative values of the leading features in numerical terms. This is not an easy thing to do and, when done, is but an expression of opinion. While seeking to omit nothing of importance, we have not made these scales so full of detail as to be practically unmanageable when applied to the purpose of critical judging."*

As an expression of general intent this could hardly be bettered and could well have been adopted as a guiding principle for many of the official standards subsequently drawn up.

It was soon after this period (the late 1880's and 1890's) that the various *Specialist*

Societies first came into being. Although some of the very old breeds may have had clubs devoted solely to them previously to this, few records of them remain (see *Illustrated London News* of December 12, 1846) and with the passing years they had mostly become defunct. Fanciers' societies of a more general nature, often catering for other forms of small livestock as well as cage birds, had of course been in existence for many years but it was mainly due to the upsurge of interest in the canary fancy during the last quarter of the nineteenth century, that led to the foundation of societies devoted to one breed of canary alone. It is to these specialist societies that we owe the breed standards that guide us in our hobby today.

SPECIALIST SOCIETIES

The general aims of most specialist societies can suitably be summarised as follows:
1. To maintain, and even improve upon, the standard of the breed they represent.
2. To cater for, and advise, fanciers who are interested in these breeds.
3. To publish and issue a *Standard of Excellence* and a *Scale of Points* appertaining to the breed.
4. To encourage the exhibiting of the breed.
5. To maintain a panel of competent judges who will officiate at shows and adhere to the standards as laid down.

It may prove helpful and relevant to enlarge upon each of these aspects of a specialist society's work in greater detail:

1. The appearance of any breed very rarely remains entirely static over a long period of time. Even the Lizard, our oldest and least changed variety, has shown considerable improvement over the years, as a comparison of today's leading examples with some of the old illustrations of the breed a century ago will clearly indicate. As mentioned in an earlier paragraph, the Norwich has become quite a different bird from its predecessors and the same is true, though to a lesser degree, in the case of some "younger" breeds such as the Yorkshire or the Border Fancy. Even comparatively recent creations, like the Gloster Fancy, have already achieved higher standards than were perhaps thought possible at the inception of the breed little more than half a century ago.

Earlier ideals, therefore can gradually be perfected and improved upon by the skills of breeders so that, eventually, the "Standard" tends to lag behind the progress that is being made. This being so, and provided that the general consensus of opinion among the adherents of any particular breed recognises and accepts the fact, then the standard is usually amended and brought up to date. Naturally there will be some fanciers who disapprove and wish to cling to the older standard but, inevitably, the majority prevails and progress continues.

As an example of this, at first many of the older Yorkshire breeders could not bring themselves to accept the new type of bird that was emerging in the post-war years, but nowadays, for every fancier who dislikes the shape of the modern Yorkshire, there are hundreds who thoroughly approve and are bringing their stocks towards new standards of perfection.

Fortunately, any changes to the official standards do not occur with any great frequency, nor merely at the whim of a few fanciers with "advanced" ideas and so those that are presented within the pages of this book, not only represent the latest and most up-to-date version in each case, but are likely to remain so for many years to come.

2. Although some of our specialist societies are organised on a regional basis, many more are entirely nationwide in their coverage and so it is only at their Annual General Meetings that members are able to meet each other and their officers in person. In order to cater for these scattered members, therefore, and to keep them informed of the various "happenings" in their section of the canary fancy, the breed societies usually adopt the method of issuing various forms of literature that are sent out by post. At the very least this consists of an annual "Year Book", or "Handbook", in which are published the society's Rules, Audited Accounts, Chairman's Annual Report, Directory of Members, and so on. There is usually also a report on the previous season's show results, together with the names of the various trophy winners, etc. More importantly, especially from the point of view of the newcomer, there is generally a reprint of the breed "Standard" so that it is always on hand for ready reference. In addition there may also be an illustration of the ideal bird and the specifications and diagrams of the official show cage.

Many societies also keep in touch with their members by means of half-yearly or quarterly Newsletters which frequently contain, not only official news items, but also articles of an informative, and sometimes controversial nature from some of the "experts". There may also be letters from members, replies to queries and so forth. Canary breeding is essentially a hobby that is carried out in the privacy of one's home, and so a lively society is one that keeps in touch with its members in every possible way in order to ensure the necessary maintenance of interest if their particular breed is to continue to flourish.

3. Turning now to the all-important Standards of Excellence with which this book is principally concerned, these of course are issued as a guide for all breeders of any given variety of canary in order to show them as clearly as possible the ideals for which they should aim. To achieve this purpose three different methods may be employed: (a) a detailed *written description* of the ideal bird, (b) a *scale of points* evaluating the salient show features and their relative values, and (c) a *pictorial representation* of the model bird.

Clearly, as a counsel of perfection, a combination of all three methods must come nearest to accomplishing its purpose by leaving as little a margin of doubt in the mind as possible. However, not all specialist societies do this, many of them merely having a written description plus a scale of points and one, in fact, (the Crested Canary Club) having a written description *only* with neither a scale of points nor a pictorial model by way of reinforcement. In this book the artist has based his paintings closely upon the official pictorial models, where these exist, or upon the written descriptions, in combination with living examples of the breed, where they do not. In this way the reader should obtain as accurate a visual impression as is possible — apart of course from studying leading examples of each breed in the form of live specimens.

4. To promote the exhibiting of their particular breed of canary each specialist society must do its utmost to encourage as many members as possible to show their birds as often as possible. This, incidentally, provides good publicity for the breed and is a useful recruiting ground for new members. Very few of the societies, however, are

1.1 Example of a Pictorial Standard issued a Specialist Society (Norwich Canary)
The original plate is in colour and was painted by the well-known canary artist the late R.A. Vowles.

large enough nor sufficiently affluent to enable them to stage their own shows (which are often quite a large and financially hazardous undertaking). The majority, therefore, have an arrangement which is known in the fancy as *Patronage Shows,* whereby they give their "patronage" to certain selected Open Shows of a general nature, catering for all branches of the cage bird fancy, and in return their members agree to support these shows with their entries. Such an arrangement benefits both the specialist society (which is spared the expense of staging its own shows) and the show promoting society (which thereby gains additional entries).

At a patronage show, the specialist society's rules and classification apply and usually some of their trophies and monetary "specials" are put up for competition as an inducement to their members to participate. In addition to the patronage shows, one show each season is selected to stage the *Club Show* in which an even greater degree of participation is expected, and usually given, by the members. This event becomes the highlight of the society's year, attracting a large entry from the really dedicated fanciers who are thus able to meet and discuss the exhibits and the important issues of the past season.

5. It is, of course, quite useless to have all the foregoing organisation unless at the end of it all there are a number of competent judges who know what they are looking for and are able to interpret the breed standard to a degree of correctness that will satisfy even the most critical of exhibitors. To this end, each specialist society has a list of approved judges, known as the *Judges Panel,* from which one or more, according to the size of the show, will be appointed to officiate at any given event.

The judges panel is the responsibility of the specialiest society's *Judging Sub-Committee* who may add to, or delete, individuals from the list as may be found necessary. Ideally, one at least of this sub-committee should be present at the show to keep an eye on, and report upon, the standard of judging to be seen — especially in the case of a judge who is fairly new to the panel. Some specialist societies have trainee judging schemes whereby an aspiring judge may serve an "apprenticeship" under one or more of the experienced old hands at the job until sufficient competence has been achieved to enable him to be recommended to the judging sub-committee. Some societies even insist upon a written examination as well — but many merely appoint any breeder who wishes to become a judge, provided that he has had a fairly long experience with the breed and has been a consistently successful exhibitor, thereby demonstrating that he at least has a good "eye" and knows what the ideal bird should look like.

ACHIEVING THE STANDARD

There is, of course, no magic formula for producing exhibition birds which match up closely to the ideal that is laid down in the standard. All practical fanciers of any experience will confirm that livestock breeding is still more of an art than a science, although science does have an increasingly important part to play — as witness the role of the geneticist in commercial livestock breeding.

It should be remembered that the various breeds of canary were originally produced by means of simple selection on a visual basis and this method, accompanied by necessity or design by a certain amount of inbreeding, led eventually to a state of reasonable genetic stability being reached, and so a recognisable type of bird emerged which "bred true" to a fairly reliable degree. Today's fancier still has to rely upon similar principles. Sound visual selection is probably still his most important single tool for, unless he knows what he is looking for and can distinguish the shades of difference between good, very good and excellent, little progress can be expected.

Pairing his best birds together and ruthlessly rejecting anything mediocre is obviously a good starting point. Then the retention of only the very best of the progeny in order to continue the process should ensure that standards are at least being maintained. Most breeders appreciate this much and work more or less on these lines, although there is often a tendency to retain too many pairs of reasonably good birds rather than to keep fewer pairs of really excellent ones. This may well guard against the disappointment of the occasional poor breeding season but usually results in far too many "average" birds being produced.

The more successful breeders often succeed in building up strains of outstanding quality which are the result of their basic sound judgment in selecting their breeding pairs aided by one or more of the following well-defined methods of livestock breeding:

1. **Inbreeding.** In order to maintain the high qualaity of his stock a fancier will often mate together closely related individuals which he knows, or can assume to be, of similar hereditary constitution. This involves the pairing of father to daughter, mother to son, brother to sister, and so on, and in favourable circumstances it may be continued for many generations. Inbreeding, however, needs to be approached with caution for, besides the establishment and renforcement of any desirable show points, it also tends to bring to light any hidden bad points that might not at first have been known to be present in the strain. This in itself is no bad thing *provided* that the faulty individuals are rigorously eliminated from any further breeding programmes.

tility and any birds possessing such weaknesses must also be discarded from any future work. Clearly, if a bird is bred that is a superb show specimen but is also plagued with weak stamina and poor fertility, the hazards and disappointments of inbreeding immediately become apparent and it requires tremendous will power to discard such a bird from the breeding room. It has happened, too often perhaps, that strains of birds have been developed which, although producing excellent show specimens, have eventually died out as a result of this inbred lack of stamina.

As a final word, inbreeding should *Never* be embarked upon with foundation stock of only moderate quality for, at best, you will only be perpetuating mediocrity.

2. **Linebreeding.** This term has often been loosely applied over the years so that it has come to have several connotations and may mean different things to different fanciers. It may be (a) a modified form of inbreeding which involves the mating of less closely related individuals such as cousins, or uncle to niece, nephew to aunt, and so on, (b) the establishment of a direct line of descent from a particularly outstanding individual by mating him first to his own daughters and then to the resulting granddaughters, etc. so that there is an increasing percentage of the original "blood" (i.e. genes) in the strain, or (c) running several separate and distinct family lines within a stud so that whenever an outcross is needed it can be done with known material from one of the other lines, thus avoiding the necessity of introducing an "unknown quantity" from elsewhere.

It will be noted that all of these methods are modified forms of inbreeding, varying only in degree, so that the same advantages and pitfalls are attendant upon their use.

3. **Outbreeding.** This consists of breeding from unrelated, or only distantly related, stock and introducing fresh blood every year or so in order to ensure that no inbreeding takes place. This system is generally held to produce a more vigorous progeny but, of course, a genuine "strain" of birds cannot be built up in this way. Fanciers who are not too concerned with the implications of various breeding theories find that outbreeding serves their purpose very well. If the initial stock, and the regular replacements, are of high quality some perfectly reasonable show specimens can usually be expected — and even with the occasional prospect of a really outstanding one.

It is not the intention of this book to go into the realms of heredity and the genetics of the canary. This subject has been dealt with elsewhere in sufficient detail for most fanciers — notably in my own book *Canaries* (Arco Publications, 1968) and its American counterpart *Encyclopedia of Canaries* (T.F.H. Publications, Inc., 1976). In the special context of the numerous mutations in the colour canary section of the fancy there is G.B.R. Walker's book *Coloured Canaries* (Blandford Press, 1976). Several other books dealing with the genetics involved in livestock breeding in general are also available and, for any fancier who wishes to go more deeply into the subject, the basic precepts contained in these apply equally to canaries.

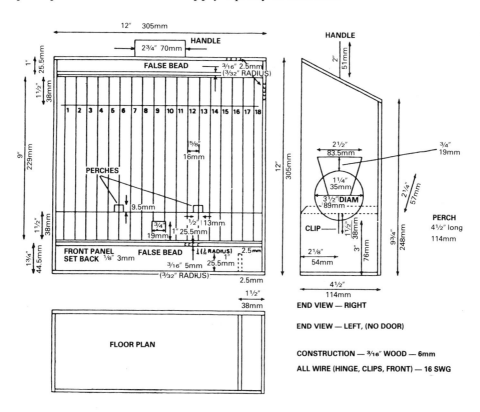

1.2   Example of Show Cage Specifications as issued by a Specialist Society

Chapter 2

EXHIBITING CANARIES

In the canary fancy it is obviously the **breeding season** which forms the basis upon which all the year's subsequent activities depend and naturally the fancier must concentrate all of his efforts into this period, which in Britain, extends from about the end of March or early April until mid-July. Having, hopefully, raised a reasonable number of youngsters and safely passed them through the successive phases of weaning, moulting and training it is the **show season** that becomes the ultimate goal of the canary fancier — or at least it should do.

The continued development and perfecting of our exhibition types of canary thrives upon the competition afforded by the showbench in exactly the same way as any other "fancy" such as the exhibition flowers which we can see at the annual horticultural shows held in towns and villages throughout the land during the summer months. It would be a pity for all these splendid blooms to "blush unseen" in somebody's back garden, or merely to be admired by the fortunate few friends who happen to drop by for a chat. It may well have given the gardener an enormous amount of pleasure in the production of his choice blossoms but, he is even better rewarded in the sharing of his achievements in competition with others through the medium of the showbench!

It is exactly the same case with our exhibition breeds of canary; it is little use having a birdroom full of potential prizewinners if nobody else sees them and so every fancier almost has a **duty** to put them out on the showbench at the appropriate season. In Britain this occupies practically every weekend from about mid-October until January during which time hundreds of shows are held up and down the country. They may range from relatively small local events up to the large National Exhibitions of England and Scotland and so the exhibitor will need to know something of the nature of the competition that is involved in the various categories.

TYPES OF SHOW

1. **Annual Members' Shows.** Entries to these shows is restricted to members of the society only and no "outsider" can exhibit. Often there is only a nominal qualifying period of (usually) a fortnight before any newly-joined member becomes eligible. In small provincial towns the number of birds exhibited may be fairly limited, perhaps three or four hundred, but in the case of flourishing societies with a large membership there may well be a thousand or more. In addition to their main annual show these local societies usually stage a "pairs" show in February and a "young stock" show in July, both of which provide plently of interest and can be most useful and instructive, especially for the beginner.

2. **Open Shows.** These are promoted and organised by various local cage bird societies, either instead of, or in addition to, their own members' annual fixture. In these shows entries are accepted from fanciers anywhere in the country without mem-

bership being a condition for participation (this is the meaning of "Open", i.e. entry is open to anybody) and so, in general, the competition is likely to be much more searching than at local level. Most of the better Open Shows receive entries of between 1500 and 2000 birds, although not all of them are as well supported as this. The large "National" shows previously referred to, of course, fall into this category and entries may well be three or four times the numbers quoted above.

3. **Specialist Societies' Shows.** As stated in the previous chapter, few of the Specialist Societies are large enough, and financially sound enough to be able to stage their own shows and so have to resort to the arrangement known as "Patronage", the workings of which have already been described. These shows are a very important part of the exhibition programme of the specialist canary breeder.

CATEGORIES OF EXHIBITOR

In Britain, classes are provided for two categories of exhibitor, namely the **Novice** and the **Champion,** and any newcomer to the canary fancy is entitled to commence his career as an exhibitor in the Novice section before graduating to Champion status. Unfortunately, the various specialist societies tend to differ somewhat in their "Novice Rule" although, clearly, it would be helpful to all concerned if the canary fancy were to adopt a ruling acceptable to all sections. In an imperfect world, however, perhaps it is too much to expect unanimity upon such a relatively simple matter!

Nevertheless, certain elements seem to be common to most clubs and a fairly widely accepted definition of a Novice is as follows: —

"A Novice exhibitor is one who, at the commencement of the show season, has not yet won three first prizes in Novice classes in Open Competition. Wins in classes with less than three exhibitors and seven staged exhibits shall not count, neither shall wins in Selling classes nor at events where the competition is not fully open. An exhibitor who commences the season as a Novice may continue to show throughout the season in that category irrespective of the number of wins gained."

There is usually a rider to the effect that, "Two or more exhibitors residing at the same address, if showing the same variety of canary, shall adopt the status of the higher one of them." This is for the obvious reason of preventing a Novice from borrowing a Champion's birds to show as his own.

Finally, it must be remembered that a Novice is not **compelled** to remain a Novice all his life if he fails to succeed in meeting the terms of the ruling above. He may move up to the senior status at any time he may choose and many novices, in fact, do this after serving, say, five or six years' apprenticeship in the hobby. Some specialist societies actually include in their rule the provision that a novice **must** move up to champion classes after a specified period. It should also, perhaps, be added that to change one's breed does not entitle him to start again as a novice with another one! "Once a Champion, always a Champion", is the understood rule in the canary world.

CLASSIFICATION

In any form of hobby, some kind of classification of the subject matter is necessary to bring order out of chaos and make the pursuit intelligible to its devotees. In the canary fancy classification is based upon age, sex, colour and markings so that there is a whole range of recognised categories which cover every type of bird that is likely to be encountered. In the table which follows the full classification is laid out in which all of the technical terms are listed and these will be described in further detail afterwards.

CLASSIFICATION OF CANARIES

Age	Sex	Colour	Markings*
Flighted	Cocks	Yellow	Clear Ticked Marked Variegated Foul Self
		Buff	Clear Ticked Marked Variegated Foul Self
	Hens	Yellow	Clear Ticked Marked Variegated Foul Self
		Buff	Clear Ticked Marked Variegated Foul Self
Unflighted	Classification is the same as for flighted birds		

*It is, in fact, rare for the full classification to be used, even at the largest shows, where **Clear and Ticked** usually compete together, also **Marked and Variegated,** and likewise **Foul and Self.**

Note: This classification is almost universal but does not apply to Lizard Canaries and certain other breeds (e.g. The Lancashire, where only clear birds are recognised on the showbench.)

Age. Upon leaving the nest at the age of three weeks young canaries are fully fledged and provided with a set of feathers that will clothe them until their first moult begins. At this stage of their lives they are known as "nest feather" birds. During the first moult, which commences when they are about 10 to 12 weeks old, the whole of these temporary nest feathers are replaced, *with the important exception of* the flight feathers of the wing and the tail feathers and the birds are then referred to as "unflighted" (i.e. their flight feathers have not been moulted).

During the following year's moult, *all* feathers are renewed including the wings and tail, and the canary then becomes a "flighted" bird. This process of feather replacement is repeated annually but there are no further special terms employed and, however old a bird may become, it is still a flighted specimen. In some sections of the fancy the term "overyear" is employed as an alternative to "flighted".

The reason for separating flighted and unflighted birds in the schedule is that the younger birds are usually at a slight disadvantage when compared with the older specimens which have had an extra year in which to develop, and this is particularly noticeable in the larger breeds such as Norwich, Yorkshires or Parisian Frills, and the crested varieties such as the Crest and the Lancashire.

Sex. As with the case of age difference, hens would be at a minor disadvantage if shown against the opposite sex. Cocks are mainly rather better in colour than their counterparts, e.g. a yellow cock is a deeper and richer yellow than a yellow hen, and a buff cock shows more colour and has less dense frosting than a buff hen; the difference may be slight but it could tell against a hen in close competition. Similarly cocks tend to have a bolder manner and more jaunty carriage then do hens — again often quite a subtle difference, but detectable by the experienced fancier.

In many of our "type" breeds, however, colour in itself carries very little weight and so it is not unusual to find a hen occasionally "walking away" with the special for Best of Breed.

Since it is often quite difficult to be able to sex a bird *with certainty* by visual appraisal, it is only by his song that a cock bird will betray himself on the showbench. Thus if, by accident or design, an exhibitor has entered a cock in a class for hens and the bird is seen by the judge to be singing, he will have no option but to pass it over.

COLOUR

In the canary there are two basic types of feather quality to be found which are known to fanciers as *yellow* and *buff*. Both types, of course, actually are yellow but in the buff birds the yellow pigment is less intense than in the yellows and does not extend quite to the extreme margin of feathers, where the absence of colouring results in a narrow edging of white. This gives to the bird a lightly frosted, or mealy, appearance which, as we have seen, is usually more accentuated in hens than in cocks. In dark pigmented birds, e.g. greens, the buff type is recognisable by again being somewhat duller in colour than the yellow and by having a greyish, or silvery, edging to the feather.

Apart from these differences in pigmentation, there are slight structural differences too, those of the buffs being somewhat larger, broader and softer in texture. This tends to make the buff generally a little bolder and "fuller" in figure, although in birds of exceptional quality the difference may be slight.

In the Coloured Canary section of the fancy the continental nomenclature has been adopted so that yellows are known as *"intensive"* and buffs as *"non-intensive"*. However, in some schedules, the older terms of "non-frosted" and "frosted" occasionally persist. In Lizard Canaries the yellows are termed *"gold"* and the buffs are known as *"silver"*.

Unfortunately, in certain breeds, there is a tendency for some yellows to carry quite a bit of mealing — sometimes to such an extent that it has led to argument as to whether the bird was a yellow or a buff! Clearly, any such "halfway stagers" are to be avoided, otherwise the fault is liable to be perpetuated. Certainly on the showbench the aim should always be to stage birds (whether yellow or buff) that are good examples of their type.

Before turning to the definitions of the various forms of marking, it should be explained that the colouring of the canary's plumage is the result of the blending of certain pigments which are present within the feather structure. In normal canaries (i.e. unmutated forms) they are three in number, namely yellow, black and brown, and various combinations of these give rise to the different types about to be described.

The basic yellow colouring, which is technically known as *lipochrome*, forms the ground colour of the plumage upon which the other pigments may, or may not, be superimposed and, as we have seen, it may occur in the two forms of yellow and buff. It extends fairly evenly throughout the web of the feather but is not present in the underflue. In the Red Canary series there is an additional lipochrome pigment of red which, combined with the yellow, gives varying shades of orange in the plumage. In the case of white canaries the lipochrome is lacking altogether, being either absent or supressed, and thus giving rise to the recessive and dominant whites — two quite distict mutations, although visually almost similar.

The two dark pigments of black and brown *(eumelanin* and *phaeomelanin)* are by no means evenly distributed, even in the case of the self green canary with its "unbroken" plumage. In this type of bird various shades of colouring can be distinguished ranging from rich, bright green, through duller green until almost verging on bronze, while the wing and tail feathers and the central shafts of the body feathers are almost black. Although the underflue contains no lipochrome, it may be coloured by the melanins and, in the case of green birds, is dark grey.

In the common mutant form of canary known to fanciers as the **Cinnamon,** the black pigments are absent leaving only the brown which, superimposed upon the yellow ground colour, produces the so-called cinnamon colouring. Very many mutations have occurred in the melanin pigments and these have been cultivated by fanciers in the Coloured Canary section of the hobby although they are virtually unknown in the type breeds.

The green canary alluded to above possesses the full complement of pigmentation with no light feathering present at all — exactly the same, in fact, as the original wild canary when it was first domesticated. As happens with most species of birds or animals under the influence of domestication, the plumage of the canary began to break up in course of time into pied, or broken patterns, many of which were described by the French writer, Hervieux, as long ago as 1709. The breaking up of the plumage pattern continued progressively until it culminated in the complete disappearance of all the melanins leaving the familiar clear yellow bird. Thus, between the self green on the one hand and the clear yellow on the other, there exists a whole range of broken patterned birds, the diverse markings of which form the basis for the classification shown in the table and which are now defined below.

CLEAR

In the clear, there should be no dark feathering present at all so that the bird is quite recognisable as either a clear yellow, or a clear buff, as previously described. Very occasionally, an otherwise clear bird may possess a certain amount of dark pigmentation in the underflue (the soft, fluffy part of the feather next to the skin) but, so long as it is not seen on the surface as the bird stands on its perch, it is generally acceptable as a clear. Any little dark markings on the beak, legs or feet are usually disregarded in the definition of a clear bird.

TICKED

Certain specialist societies have their own standard concerning what constitutes a ticked bird but, for the majority, the generally accepted definition of a tick is, "A *single* area of dark feathers occurring anywhere on the body of the bird and not exceeding a one penny piece in size *OR*, one wing or tail mark consisting of not more than *three adjacent* dark feathers, which thus form a single mark". The latter, it should be noted, might well exceed a one penny piece in size since the mark would be linear rather than rounded. As with all forms of marking, there are bound to be some borderline cases over which the judge will naturally exercise his discretion, usually leaning towards tolerance unless the bird is clearly well beyond the limits of the definition.

MARKED

These kinds of marking are officially referred to by fanciers as "Technical" marks and are applied specifically to markings that are limited to three areas of the body only and nowhere else. They are the eyes, the secondary flight feathers of the wings, and the outer tail feathers. According to how these markings may be disposed, a bird may be either *evenly* or *unevenly* marked and is designated two-pointed, four-pointed or six-pointed if the marks are evenly balanced, or three-pointed or five-pointed if uneven. The possession of just one of these technical marks, it should be noted, would usually constitute a ticked bird as defined in the foregoing paragraph.

In the past, these technically marked birds were very much admired in the fancy — to the extent that separate classes were at one time provided for them at the shows, as distinct from the ordinary run of irregularly marked specimens. They are indeed most attractive birds to look at, although nowadays no particular importance is attached to them, *type* always being the major consideration in most breeds. Thus in the present-day shows they have to take their place alongside the general run of variegated birds. Care should be taken, however, in entering Yorkshire canaries as this section of the fancy still makes use of technical markings in its official terminology.

EXAMPLES OF TICKED BIRDS

(a) One body mark coverable by a
1p piece

(b) Not more than three adjacent
dark feathers in one wing

(c) Not more than three adjacent
dark feathers in the tail

These birds are not ticked

(a) Body mark too large

(b) Body marks although small enough
are two in number

(c) Too many dark feathers
in the wing

(d) Tail feathers although three in
number are not adjacent

EXAMPLES OF TECHNICAL MARKS

(a) Touching left eye

(b) Touching right eye

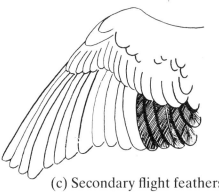

(c) Secondary flight feathers
of left wing

(d) Secondary flight feathers
of right wing

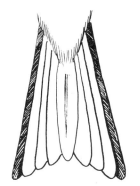

(e) Outer tail feathers

EXAMPLES OF TECHNICAL MARKS (cont.)

(f) Technically marked bird (Six pointed)

(g) This bird is *not* technically marked (i.e. mark not touching eye, wing marks not on secondary flights)

16

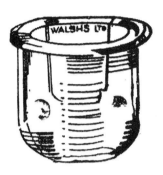

2.1   Open Glass Drinker as used for Border, Fife and Scotch Fancy Canaries

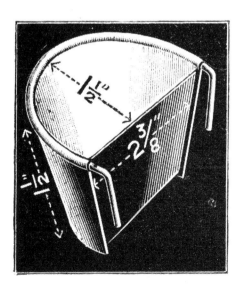

2.2   Two-Hooked Drinker in Metal or Plastic as used for all other varieties

VARIEGATED

The reader will have gathered by now that a variegated bird is one in which the plumage is broken up into mainly irregular areas of light and dark feathers. Because of the large numbers of these, for the purposes of identification, and sometimes of show classification, the variegated birds can be sub-divided into the following categories: —
lightly variegated — having less than half the plumage of a dark colour;
heavily variegated — having more than half the plumage of a dark colour;
three-parts dark — having 75% or more of the plumage of a dark colour.

FOUL

This is applied to otherwise dark plumaged birds which may have some light feathers among the flight feathers of their wings, or in their tails. There is no universal ruling on just *how many* light feathers are allowable. Three is sometimes quoted but some authorities will accept any number provided that there are no other light feathers anywhere else on the body. In practice, a large number of light feathers in the wings and tail are nearly always accompanied by areas of light feathering elsewhere, usually under the beak or in the vicinity of the abdomen, legs and vent, which would then place the bird in the category of "three parts dark". As mentioned under the heading "Ticked", there are always some borderline cases which may be difficult to classify.

SELF

A self bird is one in which the melanin pigments are present throughout the whole of its plumage with *no light feathers* anywhere to mar its perfection. In some sections of the fancy, selfs form a very important category, some, in fact, only ever being shown in the self form.

These definitions of the various kinds of marking apply in all circumstances, whatever melanin pigments or ground colours may be present, with the sole exception of Lizard Canaries whose classification will be dealt with in the section on the breed. In cinnamon birds, the markings, however, will be brown instead of green and in white canaries the equivalent colours are blue instead of green and fawn instead of cinnamon. In most show schedules usually no special classes are provided for cinnamon marked and variegated birds, and so they have to compete against the normal green marked birds, but there *may* be a separate class, or classes, for cinnamon selfs — especially in the case of Norwich Canaries where cinnamons are a well-recognised sub-variety.

White ground birds, being less widely kept than normals, are most often all lumped together under the heading "White and Allied Colours", but much depends upon the size of the show in question so that the fancier must be alert and read the schedule carefully before entering his birds.

SHOW CAGES

Unlike poultry, pigeons, rabbits, etc., where the show authorities provide the pens in which the exhibits are to be staged, the canary fancier is obliged to have his own show cages. In these his birds will be taken to the show and remain throughout its duration until brought home again.

Before the advent of specialist societies there was no uniformity in these cages, each fancier using a design that he thought displayed his birds to best advantage. Nowadays, however, show cages are completely uniform in pattern and colour, although they do vary from breed to breed. This is because each specialist society has designed a type of cage most suitable for viewing its own particular breed and these cages are the only ones now acceptable on the showbench.

Standard show cages are obtainable from most fanciers' suppliers but it is quite permissible for the enthusiast to make his own, always providing that he complies exactly with the specifications laid down. Details of these are to be found in most specialist societies' *Standards* and have been included where applicable within this book.

To transport their birds to and from the shows most fanciers provide themselves with travelling cases in which the show cages can safely be placed. Naturally they are guided by the size of their potential "show teams", but it is often convenient to have cases made to hold two, three, four and six show cages (anything larger would be too unwieldy) which, in various combinations would permit any number of birds, from two to fifteen, to be exhibited.

ENTERING

When intending to enter his birds for a show the fancier must first of all obtain a *Schedule* from the show secretary. In the case of members' shows these are usually despatched automatically but with open shows they must be sent for. During the show season all the major open events are advertised in the fancy press and all that is necessary is to contact the secretary, whose address will appear in the advertisement, asking for a schedule to be forwarded. A careful reading of the show rules and examination of the classification should precede writing up one's entries which should be placed on the special entry form that is enclosed with the schedule. This should not be left until the last minute for, in the interests of efficient organisation, the shows have a closing date for entries to be received, after which none will be accepted.

STAGING

A few days prior to the show the cage labels, already marked with the appropriate class and cage numbers, will be received from the show secretary. These should be fixed in accordance with the rules which, in most breeds, lay down that they should be on the bottom left-hand side as the cage faces you. There are some exceptions to this, dictated by the shape of the cage, notably for the Border and Fife Fancy canaries.

It is both careless and unforgivable to stage a decent bird in a shabby or dirty cage and the true enthusiast will ensure that his exhibits have the benefit of immaculate show cages which have either been freshly painted or had any chipped paint or bare wires touched up. It is most important, too, to ensure that the pattern of the perches and the floor covering are "as per standard" for, when it comes to a close decision, a bird that has been faultlessly staged will have the advantage.

As to the preparation of the birds themselves, including show training and any hand washing or spraying that may be deemed necessary, these items are invariably dealt with at some length in most standard handbooks on canary culture and so are not included here.

JUDGING

Except in the case of the Roller Canary, which is judged by means of listening to its song and awarding points for the excellence of its delivery, in Britain the judging of all the other canaries takes place on the system of visual comparison of the exhibits. Each

2.3   Travelling Case for Show Cages
The dimensions would naturally vary according to the type and number of cages it is intended to accommodate.

class in turn is placed before the judge who then arranges the birds in order of merit according to how closely they approach the standards laid down by the specialist society. If numbers are sufficient, seven placings are made and traditionally they are first, second, third, fourth, very highly commended (V.H.C.), highly commended (H.C.) and commended (C.). There is, however, a growing tendency merely to number the awards from first to seventh and to drop the older "courtesy" titles of the lower placings.

Having dealt with all of his classes, the judge then takes all the individual winners and moves on to make the special awards — known to fanciers simply as "Specials". These usually include the categories of Best Unflighted, Best Flighted, Best Novice, Best Champion, Best of Breed, Best Opposite Sex, and so on. The final award that is generally made at most shows, and often a very controversial one, is that of Best Canary in Show which is the ultimate accolade to which every fancier aspires.

Example of Classification taken from the Schedule of an Open Show

YORKSHIRE CANARY CLASSIFICATION
JUDGE: E. MURRAY   SECTION STEWARD: R. SEARS

CHAMPION			NOVICE	
Fltd.	U/F		Fltd.	U/F
35	47	Clear, Ticked or Lightly Var. (only one technical mark) Yellow Cock	59	71
36	48	Clear, Ticked or Lightly Var. (only one technical mark) Buff Cock	60	72
37	49	Clear, Ticked or Lightly Var. (only one technical mark) Yellow Hen	61	73
38	50	Clear, Ticked or Lightly Var. (only one technical mark) Buff Hen	62	74
39	51	Green, even, uneven or var. (two or more technical marks) Self or Foul Yellow Cock	63	75
40	52	Green, even, uneven or Var. (two or more technical marks) Self or Foul Buff Cock	64	76
41	53	Green, even, uneven or Var. (two or more technical marks) Self or Foul Yellow Hen	65	77
42	54	Green, even, uneven or Var. (two or more technical marks) Self or Foul Buff Hen	66	78
43	55	Cinnamon Ticked, Marked or Var. Self or Foul Yellow or Buff Cock	67	79
44	56	Cinnamon Ticked, Marked or Var. Self or Foul Yellow or Buff Hen	68	80
45	57	White and Allied Colour Cock or Hen	69	81
46	58	Non-fed Green, Self or Foul Cock or Hen	70	82

JUNIOR YORKSHIRE
83 Any Variety Yorkshire Adult
84 Any Variety Yorkshire 1982 bred

3.0   Old-type Belgian Canary

Chapter 3

THE BELGIAN

HISTORY

Although it is now a relatively scarce breed, even in its homeland, the Belgian must still be regarded as one of the most important breeds in the history of the canary fancy. This is not only because it was a major exhibition variety during a large part of the nineteenth century, but also on account of the great influence it had upon the development of several other exhibition forms of canary.

The origins of the Belgian are unrecorded but early authorities mention the so-called "Old Dutch" canary which, as far as can be gathered, was not a well-defined breed such as might be recognised today, but a somewhat variable race of domestic canaries which existed in the Low Countries during the latter part of the eighteenth century. It would appear that from this ancestral stock several lines of descent were established which led eventually to some of our modern breeds.

In the case of the Belgian, the development and refinement of the breed proceeded with great single-mindedness of purpose aided by the "guilds" that had existed in most of the towns and cities of Belgium since medieval times. Before the middle years of the nineteenth century a highly "fancy" type of bird had been developed that fanciers regarded as the equivalent of the thoroughbred in horses. English fanciers were so impressed with it that they dubbed it "king of the fancy" and high prices were willingly paid for outstanding birds.

Its long "reign" continued almost to the end of the century by which time, however, there were already signs that the Belgian was beginning to lose some of its former support. The leading canary experts of the time attributed this to the inroads that were being made into the stocks of Belgians for the purpose of improving other breeds, notably the Scotch Fancy and the Yorkshire. For a while these losses were made good to some extent by the continued importation of fresh purebred stock from Belgium but the outbreak of the first world war put an end to this and proved to be a disaster from which the breed has never really recovered.

The four years of hostilities brought about the near extinction of the Belgian canary in its homeland although efforts made by dedicated fanciers resulted in the preservation of some remnants of the decimated stocks. After the war, by making use of some of the breeds to which the Belgian had been crossed in the past, the breed became re-established during the 1920's and 30's but the coming of the second world war dealt yet another blow.

Since 1945 the whole rescue operation has had to be repeated, but this time with very little pure blood being available, so that the present-day Belgian canary is a somewhat degenerate example of the breed as it was in its heyday. It is entirely to the credit of Belgian fanciers, however, that it exists at all and, as time goes by and the process of selection has its effect, it is to be hoped that this famous old breed of canary will be restored to something like its former glory.

The name by which the Belgian was known in the earliest days of its history *"post-uurvogel",* indicates that it was a "posture bird" or, in English, a "bird of position" and Victorian canary experts subsequently used this term to embrace the various breeds in which a specific show position was all important to display their points to best advantage. All of these possess certain bodily characteristics which together form their basic type, and these are then displayed to perfection as the bird adopts its show position.

POINTS OF THE BELGIAN

In considering the details of the breed, the Belgian must, therefore, be examined under those twin headings of "type" and "position" as, indeed, is found in the official standard.

The Belgian canary should have a small, neat head which is oval in shape and with a somewhat sleek and almost snaky appearance. The neck should be long and fine and capable of being much extended when the bird is in position. The body should be long and tapering, with a straight back ending in a tail that is long and closely folded, continuing the straight line by being stiffly held and not loose or supple to spoil the line by swinging about.

The under surface of the body also presents a line that is straight through from breast to tail so that a side elevation of the bird, taken from shoulder through to the breast and down to the tail shows it to be somewhat triangular or wedge-shaped in appearance. Indeed, it is probably not too much to describe the Belgian as a bird constructed on the principle of straight lines and angles.

Nevertheless, the truly distinctive feature which characterises this canary above all others, are its high, broad and prominenet shoulders which give it a remarkable hump-backed appearance, and it is from this peculiarity that it is known in its native land — *Belgische Bult,* or *Bossu Belge* — meaning Belgian Humpback.

The bird also has very long legs which often tend to show a good length of thigh and, moreover, they are quite straight and stiffly held with very little flexibility at the "elbow" joint. This characteristic, together with the bird's natural "nerve" enable it to assume its correct posture in the show cage.

To do this it grips the perch firmly with its feet and pulls itself erect and up to its fullest possible height, at which point the line of the back from shoulder to the tip of the tail should be completely perpendicular. At the same time as the shoulders are being raised, the head and neck are actually being lowered, with the neck stretched out to its limit and the bird looking downwards with its beak pointing to the floor of the cage. This typical position, which thus forms something resembling a figure seven, can be held by the bird for several seconds at a time while the judge assesses its merits and, generally speaking, the higher the shoulders and the lower the head the more the bird is thought of. As many as 40 points out of 100 are allowed in the standard for the bird's position and so it is clearly a most important feature of the breed.

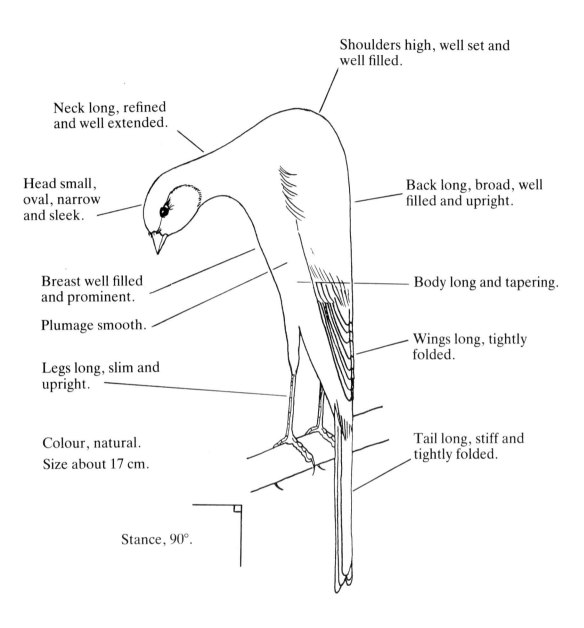

Shoulders high, well set and well filled.

Neck long, refined and well extended.

Head small, oval, narrow and sleek.

Back long, broad, well filled and upright.

Breast well filled and prominent.

Plumage smooth.

Body long and tapering.

Wings long, tightly folded.

Legs long, slim and upright.

Colour, natural. Size about 17 cm.

Tail long, stiff and tightly folded.

Stance, 90°.

3.1   The Points of a Belgian Canary

EXHIBITING THE BELGIAN

As the Belgian is essentially a highly developed exhibition variety, it is clear that proper training to encourage it to give of its best is an important part of show preparation. Individual birds will be found to vary a good deal in their willingness to "display" although the old-fashioned thoroughbred would do this almost as soon as put into his show cage. Fortunate indeed is the fancier whose stock is possessed of a high degree of intelligence and with the inherited ability to adopt the characteristic posture but, at the same time, no despair need be felt over any "slow learners" as, provided sufficient patience is exercised, they may eventually be just as good in the show cage as their brighter companions.

As with all canaries, the early stages of training are the same and what follows need not be repeated in subsequent chapters.

SHOW TRAINING

The early stages of show training are virtually the same for all breeds of canary and the matter is usually dealt with in most of the standard textbooks that have been published. However, since it is particulary relevant to the subject of the present book, details are included in the following paragraphs before proceeding to the special needs of the Belgian.

The first essential is to familiarise the young birds with their show cages. This begins only a week or so after they have been weaned by hanging the show cages on the front of the stock cage with the two doors open and opposite to each other. The young birds' curiosity will soon cause them to explore and new environment and eventually they will spend most of the day hopping in and out, often spending a lot of the day there. At this stage it is preferable to remove the show cage each evening and replace it again every morning.

No futher action need be taken until the youngsters are about eight weeks old at which time they can be encouraged to enter the show cage on demand. This can be achieved by introducing a long thin stick into the stock cage and gently guiding them towards the door of the show cage. Running them into a show cage is an essential part of their training and much patience may be needed before some birds will do so willingly. If they are reluctant to enter, it can often help if an old bird, who knows what is expected, is included in the exercise and the youngsters will learn by example. In due time, even the stick may not be required to indicate what is wanted and a really well trained bird will immediately hop into its show cage as soon as it is offered to it.

Here it should be stressed that show Belgians should never be caught up by hand and placed into a show cage as it may, at the very least, make them nervous and, at worst, so frightened that they may be quite spoiled for exhibition.

The next stage is to take the show cage away with the young bird inside it and this, again, must be done very gently indeed to avoid alarming the youngster. No more need be done than to place the cage quietly on a table or training bench in the birdroom and allow the bird to settle down by ignoring it and going about the normal birdroom tasks. Three or four trainees can, with advantage, be dealt with at the same time so that seeing each other in a similar situation will prove to be reassuring and they will rapidly settle and gain in confidence.

After running the youngsters out in this manner for several days, and allowing them to remain out for longer periods each day, a start may be made in handling the cages and teaching the young Belgians to go into position. Needless to say, this requires a great deal of skill, patience and ingenuity.

The usual methods advised in canary manuals can be used as a basis for this stage of the training, such as gently scratching the bottom of the cage with the fingernail to attract the bird's attention and make it alert. Then the cage may be held up high to make the bird look down and, when used to this sort of handling, a thin cane, pencil or juding stick can be inserted between the wires of the cage at a point below and from behind the bird. This should have the effect of causing it to pull its shoulders up to their full height and stretch its head down to look at the stick from underneath its own legs. Eventually it will learn that this is the position required as soon as the cage is handled and any further inducement will not be required.

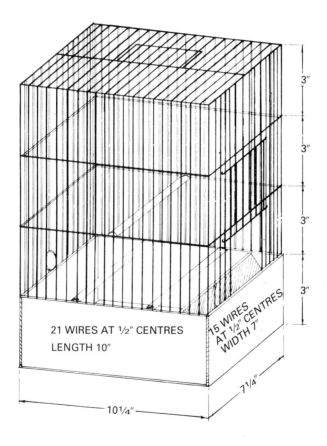

3.2 Show Cage for Belgian and Frilled Canaries

As with all forms of training, this should not be overdone otherwise the bird may eventually become "stale" and be slow, or even cease, to react. On the showbench it should, of course, be alert and hightly active as soon as handled by the judge who naturally cannot spend unlimited time on reluctant performers.

The show cage used for Belgian canaries in Great Britain is of the open wire type with a flat top and an all wooden base. The cage measures 10 inches long, 7 inches wide and 12 inches high, of which the wooden base accounts for the bottom 3 inches. It is enamelled black throughout and has a black, hook-on type of show cage drinker either in metal or plastic. The drinker hole is in the front (narrow) side of the cage and the door on the opposite end, with a seed trough just inside.

The three perches are of a plain oval section although no precise dimensions are laid down and so the fancier should experiment until he finds out what size suits his birds best to enable them to take a proper grip and stand up with confidence.

OFFICIAL STANDARD

The standard applied for the judging of Belgian canaries in the United Kingdom is the same as that laid down by the European organisation known as the Confederation Ornithologique Mondiale (C.O.M.). It is as follows —

1. **Posture**   points
   Position: Comfortable and confident.   10
   Neck: Fine and well elongated.   10
   Legs: Upright and stiff.   4
   Shoulders: High.   10
   Head: Lowered.   6
2. **Form.**
   Head: Small, oval, narrow and sleek.   3
   Neck: Long, refined and extended.   10
   Shoulders: High, well set and well filled   10
   Back: Long, broad, well filled and upright.   5
   Body: Long and tapering.   5
   Breast: Prominent and well filled.   5
   Wings: Long, tightly folded and touching without crossing.   5
   Tail: Long, upright, closely folded, stiff and closed at the tip. 3
   Legs: Long, slim and upright.   4
   Plumage: Smooth, without frills.   6
   Size: 17 to 18 cm. from the tip of the beak to the end of the tail. 4

Total 100

At present, there is only one specialist society in Great Britain that caters for the Belgian canary and this is the **Old Varieties Canary Association.**

Chapter 4

THE BORDER FANCY

This is the most popular breed of canary at the present time but, so far as the long history of the canary fancy is concerned, it is not a particularly ancient one. It was not even mentioned in the great standard works on canaries written in Victorian times; not, that is, until the third edition of R.L. Wallace's *The Canary Book* which was published in 1893. In the introduction of this edition, the author stated that he had revised and brought his work up-to-date by the inclusion of "particulars of the variety now known as the Border Fancy". By the time the first world war had broken out, the Border had become well established and books on canaries that were written in the first decade of the century contained a full treatment of the breed along with the older established varieties.

The origins of the breed lay in the ordinary common canary that was widely kept by fanciers on either side of the Anglo-Scottish border, which is the particular "Border" referred to in the title. These birds were gradually improved in type, then standardised as an exhibition form, and the first specialist society to cater for them was established in 1890 when the present name of the breed was adopted. The epithet "Fancy" also appears in the names of several other British breeds, the connotation being a specially cultivated *show* type as opposed to the common or garden variety as, for example, in the "fancy" pansies and other show flowers in the horticultural world. (The Oxford Dictionary defines *fancy* in this connection as, "bred for particular points of beauty, based upon complicated or arbitrary qualifications.")

The Border of those early days was a small, neat, active little bird which, in appearance, was not unlike the Fife Fancy of today; and so it remained for almost half a century, being affectionately known in the canary fancy as the "wee gem". In the immediate post-war years after the second world war, Borders began to grown in size, clearly with the aid of "outside" blood (probably Norwich) and the larger bird soon began to find favour with breeders and judges alike. Although some reaction to this has subsequently set in, modern Borders are still quite a size larger than their forbears (many of them much *too* large some critics would say) and they also differ in some details from the original conception of the breed, although most of the primary ideals are still of great importance.

It has often been said, and with a great deal of truth, that the Border is an ideal beginner's bird. In case it should be thought that there is an implication of them being "easy" in this remark, it must be pointed out that top quality specimens are just as difficult to achieve as in any other breed of canary. What is meant is that Borders are always readily available from pet shops, dealers or local breeders; they are hardy and vigorous birds and, in general, are trouble-free breeders so that the beginner is likely to be faced with few problems at the outset of his fancying career.

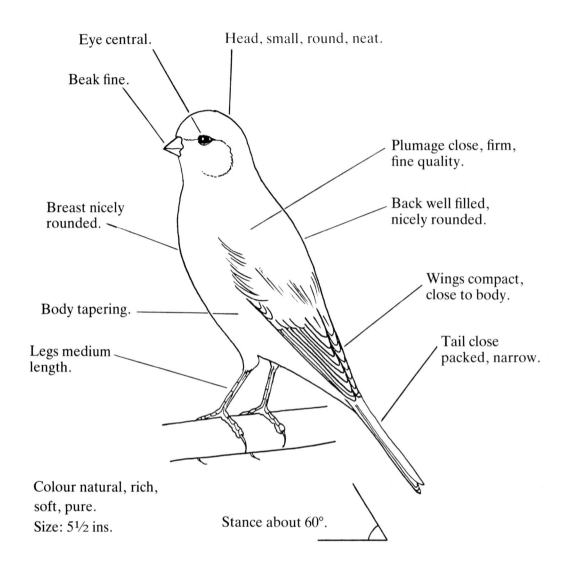

Eye central.

Head, small, round, neat.

Beak fine.

Plumage close, firm, fine quality.

Back well filled, nicely rounded.

Breast nicely rounded.

Body tapering.

Wings compact, close to body.

Legs medium length.

Tail close packed, narrow.

Colour natural, rich, soft, pure.
Size: 5½ ins.

Stance about 60°.

4.1   The Points of a Border Fancy Canary

Since its inception the Border has gone from strength to strength as its popularity has increased and now has devotees that run into many thousands all over the world wherever canaries are kept.

POINTS OF THE BORDER CANARY

In certain of our breeds of canary some characteristics have been developed to a very high degree — in fact, in some eyes, to unreasonable limits but "beauty is in the eye of the beholder" and, perhaps, the general public's idea of what a canary should look like is epitomised in the Border Fancy. That is to say that it has no eye-catching peculiarities such as a crest, or frilled feathering, or an unusual posture, but is a plain, neat, straightforward, evenly-balanced bird in which no particular feature predominates.

In general terms, it should at once create an impression of complete symmetry with perfect proportions in all of its parts. The head should be neat and round with a bright, alert eye centrally placed and a fine smallish beak. The neck should be properly proportioned, in relation to the head and body and should never be short and thick, nor too long and fine, either extreme being equally a fault.

The body should be well rounded and compact and, after a nice rise over the shoulders, the back should taper gradually away in a straight line towards the root of the tail. The breast and underparts should also be gracefully rounded in one continuous curve, but not unduly prominent, and again taper off cleanly between the legs to the underside of the tail.

The tail itself should be shortish and narrow, with the feathers closely compacted, and should continue precisely the meeting of the lines from the back and underparts. It should always be firmly held, neither too high nor too low, and should not droop or swing about. The wings, also shortish, should be carried tightly braced and close to the body with the primaries meeting neatly at the tips and not overlapping or crossing each other; neither should they fail to meet, thus leaving the feathers of the rump exposed.

In keeping with all the other features, the legs should be of moderate length and show nothing of the thigh joints. They should support the bird in a semi-upright position of about 60 degrees from the horizontal. The Border should be a free and easy mover, passing from perch to perch with balance, neither pitching forward nor having to steady itself repeatedly, and demonstrating a sprightly and jaunty manner in so doing.

In addition to its beautifully balanced proportions, this canary is renowned for its suberb feather quality, the plumage of a top-class show specimen being close, short and fine. This provides a perfect finish to a well-proportioned bird and any suggestion of poor quality of feathering should be quite out of the question.

In Victorian times the practice was introduced of **colour feeding** some varieties of canary for show purposes which is still continued to this day. This has the effect of turning an otherwise yellow bird into some shade of orange and certainly enhances the appearance of those varieties upon which it is still practised. In the case of the Border, however, from the very first colour feeding was discouraged and a decision to ban its use was made after a referendum of breeders in 1901. To this day the breed is still

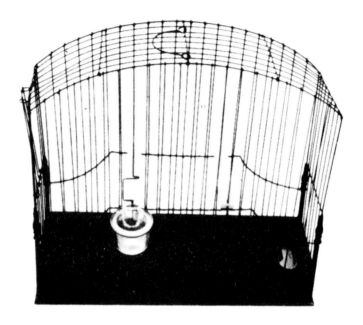

Dimensions:
Length 12³⁄₁₆ inches (30.9cm) *Width* 4¾ inches (12.06cm)
Height 11 inches (27.9cm) at ends 9 inches (22.8cm)
Base ³⁄₃₂ inches (24mm) thick
Bottom rail 1³⁄₈ inches (3.5cm) by ³⁄₁₆ inch (47mm)
Corner posts 3¼ inches (8.25cm) by ³⁄₁₆ inch (47mm) square
Drawer front 1½ inches (3.6cm) by ¾ inch (1.9cm)
Handle ½ inch (1.27cm) round head screw
Drinking hole ⅞ inch (2.2cm) by ¾ inch (1.9cm)
Crossbar 4½ inches (11.4cm) from base
Frame 16 gauge wire; *Filling* 18 gauge wire
Finish to be black gloss

4.2 Border Fancy Canary Show Cage — The Dewar Pattern

shown in its natural yellow colour which, nevertheless, should always be as rich and level as possible in both buffs and yellows.

EXHIBITING THE BORDER

Being the most widely-kept canary at the present time also means that the Border is very well represented on the showbench. Indeed, at shows of any standing the competition can be quite severe, with classes of anything up to 40 or 50 birds at the major events, so clearly the fancier should leave nothing to chance in order to ensure that his birds are benched with everything in their favour. As in the case of the Belgian already dealt with in the previous chapter, this would involve careful training of the birds so that they will appear before the judge at the very peak of their form, and paying scrupulous attention to detail in matters appertaining to the showcage and its fittings as laid down by the Border specialist societies.

All of the preliminary training of the young birds is the same as that advised for the Belgian. In the later stages, however, they must be taught not only to stand up well and hold a position typical of their breed when required to do so, but also to move with a free and jaunty action across the perches. A really good Border should hop from perch to perch quite readily and with perfect balance involving neither use of the wings nor unsteadiness at the end. The bird should be trained to remain on its perches all the time it is being handled and not be continually diving down onto the bottom of the cage, nor clambering up the wires, actions which are likely to provoke little sympathy from a judge who may have two or three hundred birds to deal with in his various classes.

The type of cage in which Borders are exhibited is known as the Dewar Show Cage. It is in an open wire cage with a wooden base and is entirely painted in black. It is basically rectangular in shape, being 12¼ inches long by 4⁹⁄₁₆ inches wide, but has an arched top to it which is 9¼ inches high at the sides rising to 11¼ inches at the apex. At the left-hand end there is a 3-wire sliding door and on the opposite side on the floor there is a seed trough which is partially covered but has a slot cut in it to allow the bird access to the seed. The perches of the show cage are ⅝ inch diameter and are of a spiral pattern containing sixteen teeth which should be cut, not rolled. They have one edge bevelled which should be placed in position with the bevel facing downwards. The perches should be placed in the cage equidistant from either end and with six clear wires between them.

The usual small sized open glass drinkers are used and are fixed in position by a wire ring opposite to the left-hand perch. The drinking aperture must be formed by the appropriate wire bent in the approved manner and should never be a round one — a feature that merits disqualification at any show. Floor covering must always be of oat husks. The show cage labels are placed immediately below the perch at the far end from the drinker and should merely show the class and cage number with no other marks or labels showing. It is in the interests of the exhibitor to ensure that all details are rigidly adhered to otherwise he may find himself debarred from competing for the specialist club awards.

OFFICIAL STANDARD

The official standard of the Border Fancy is as follows: —

STANDARD OF EXCELLENCE

The grand essentials of a Border Fancy Canary are TYPE and QUALITY. Without these it is useless.

The general appearance is that of a clean-cut, lightly-made, compact, proportionable, close-feathered canary, showing no tendency to heaviness, roughness or dullness, but giving the impression of fine quality and symmetry throughout.
Points.

10 **Head** — Small, round and neat looking, beak fine, eyes central to roundness of head and body.

15 **Body** — Back well filled and nicely rounded, running in almost a straight line from the gentle rise over the shoulders to the point of the tail. Chest also nicely rounded, but neither heavy nor prominent, the line gradually tapering to the vent.

10 **Wings** — Compact and carried close to the body, just meeting at the tips, at a little lower than the root of the tail.

5 **Legs** — Of medium length, showing little thigh, fine, and in harmony with the other points, yet corresponding.

10 **Plumage** — Close, firm, fine in quality, presenting a smooth, glossy silken appearance, free from frill or roughness.

5 **Tail** — Close packed and narrow, being nicely rounded and filled in at the root.

15 **Position** — Semi-erect, standing at an angle of 60 degrees.
  Carriage — Gay, jaunty, with full poise of the head.

15 **Colour** — Rich, soft and pure, as level in tint as possible throughout but extreme depth and hardness, such as colour feeding gives are **debarred.**

10 **Health** — Condition and cleanliness shall have due weight.

5 **Size** — But not to exceed 5½ inches in length.

___
100
___

The Border Clubs then go on to give their official interpretations of the various definitions, most of which conform to the ones already given in the chapter on Exhibiting Canaries. For the benefit of Border exhibitors, however, they are repeated herewith.

DEFINITIONS

Ticked Bird
A ticked bird is as follow: A Ticked bird to carry one mark only, Dark or Grizzle, on body or head, coverable by one new penny (1p), or three dark feathers or grizzle on the wing or three dark feathers in tail, and they must be side by side to form a solid or grizzle mark, and these are not coverable by one new penny (1p).

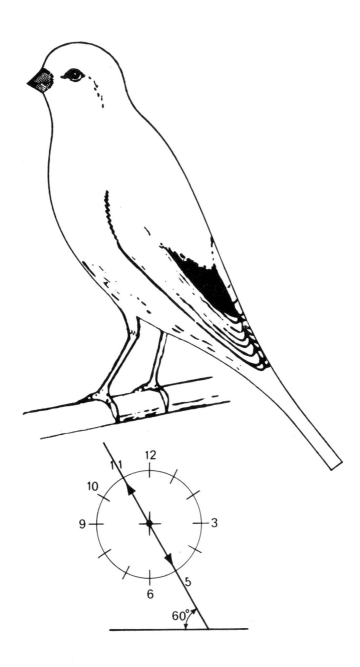

4.3   Official Pictorial Standard of the Border Fancy Canary

Special Note
Should the THREE dark feathers in either wing or tail be split, e.g. TWO dark feathers, then ONE clear feather, followed by ONE other dark feather, this would constitute a VARIEGATED BIRD. A "FOUL" Bird is opposite to a Ticked Bird.

Even Marked
An even-marked bird is one with FOUR technical marks, Viz., marks to be even on both wings and both eyes, broken marks to be disallowed. (In judging marked birds, TYPE and QUALITY should form the first consideration in these as well as in all other classes, and no prize should be awarded for good marking alone where the type does not conform to the Combined Border Clubs' Standard of Excellence).

Variegated Birds
Shall be those which have other markings in addition to, or without the technical marks, thus:
    (a) **VARIEGATED** — More light than dark
    (b) **HEAVILY VARIEGATED** — More dark than light
    (c) **THREE PARTS DARK** — To be 75 per cent dark

Self Bird
A "self" bird shall be one having no light feathers visible. Light flue under region of vent shall not merit disqualification.

Greens
The Green Border Fancy must conform to the Standard of Excellence on all points but COLOUR. The correct colour shall be of a rich grass geen, sound and level throughout, free from bronze or olive tint, pencilling on back to be clear and distinct, but neither broad nor heavy; flank pencilling to be finer, but in harmony with that on the back. Beak, Legs and feet dark; light beak, legs or feet not to be disqualification, but to count against the bird according to extent. **POINTS TO BE AVOIDED ARE:** — Head too dark, light throat or thighs, lightness on abdomen towards vent or on rump.

Cinnamons
The Cinnamon Border Fancy Canary must conform to the Standard of Excellence in all points but COLOUR. The colour to be rich, deep cinnamon throughout, with faint markings on back and flanks. Greenish or too light tints to be avoided.

    There are a great number of Border specialist societies in Great Britain alone, most of which belong to the Border Convention, an overall authority to ensure uniformity of Standards, Rules, Classification and all other matters appertaining to the breed.

Chapter 5

COLOURED CANARIES

A MODERN DEVELOPMENT

The breeding and exhibiting of coloured canaries (until recently referred to as **New** coloured canaries) is a fairly modern development in the fancy, belonging almost exclusively to the present century. In the very early days of fancying, naturally breeders were fascinated by the breaking up of the canary's wild-type plumage into the pied or variegated patterns that are common today and the earliest written work on canaries; that of the French writer Hervieux in 1709, contained a list of varieties, then known, that was entirely based on such variation. Later on, notably in the late eighteenth and early nineteenth centuries, came the development of type which led to the foundation of the various breeds of today.

Just after the turn of the present century, a mutation occurred in Holland where, among a nest of ordinary green canaries, one was seen to be very much paler in colour than the rest. About this time, too, the largely unknown work of Gregor Mendel was rediscovered and published which gave an impetus to the interest in variations from the normal, and to the modes of inheritance of various characteristics. The pale green canary was found to conform exactly to Mendelian rules of inheritance (it was a recessive, sex-linked characteristic) and was given the name **agate** by continental breeders since it was deemed to be the reappearance of a variety originally listed by Hervieux and called by him "agate".

In Britain, the new mutation was more accurately described as **dilute green** since that is exactly what it is — a dilution of the melanin pigments to something like half their normal intensity. However, in order to conform to continental practice, British coloured canary circles have recently adopted the title originally chosen and now it is "agate" over here as well so that, used in conjunction with the bird's ground colouring, we have Gold Agate (yellow ground), Silver Agate (white ground), Red Agate (red orange ground), Rose Agate (rose ground) and so on.

This dilute gene was found also to have its effect upon the brown pigments of the cinnamon canary and so the fancy soon had a **dilute cinnamon** which was called "isabel" on the continent, and this term also has now been adopted in this country. As with the Agate, it can be present with any of the lipochrome ground colours so that we have the Red Isabel, Rose Isabel, Gold Isabel, etc. Of these, the first mentioned (the Red Isabel) is one of the "classics" of the coloured canary world and is often considered to be one of the most beautiful in this section of the fancy.

The advent of the dilute mutation can thus be regarded as the starting point of an interest in canaries with unusual colours as opposed to the type breeds or the song of the Roller. Many other mutations have since occurred, among which may be mentioned white canaries (two distinct mutations, "dominant" and "recessive" white) before the first world war and, much more recently, the dimorphic, the opal, the lipochrome pastel, the melanin pastel, the satinette and the ino. Since some of these are mutations affecting the ground colour and others the melanin pigments, it can be seen that the number of possible combinations are almost endless. Unfortunately, some breeders of the casual "hit or miss" kind have completely lost track of what they have, especially in the case of the recessive mutations, but the more serious and scientific fancier, who keeps careful records, will know exactly what each of his pairings is going to produce.

By far the most important of the new colours in the canary, however, is the Red Factor, now known simply as the Red Canary. This was achieved, not as a chance mutation, but by carefully considered, deliberate breeding in an attempt to introduce genes for red pigmentation into the canary's hereditary make-up. That this was successfully accomplished can be inferred by references in an earlier paragraph and canaries with a red ground colour are, in many fanciers' eyes, the most beautiful of all the coloured birds. As the Red Canary now has the status of a major exhibition variety in this country, a separate chapter is being devoted to it later in this book.

POINTS OF THE COLOURED CANARY

Until fairly recently, this section of the fancy has been quite untroubled as to the question of type, their priority naturally being concerned with the establishment of the various new colour mutations as they arose. As larger numbers have appeared on the showbench, however, often the only means of separating them — all other things being equal — has been by reference to type. In earlier times they were certainly a rather nondescript lot, often more or less resembling the Roller canary, but the type agreed upon now is largely based upon the Border Fancy and much of the description could well apply to either variety, although the colour bird is rather smaller, being ideally about 5 inches in length.

The many colours, of course, provide a very wide field for descriptive detail and really need a specialist book on the subject (e.g. *Coloured Canaries* by G.B.R. Walker) to cover in its entirety. In general terms, however, those varieties which are normally shown as *clear* birds, i.e. Red, Rose, Ivory or White, should be good representatives of their colour as laid down by the specialist societies, each colour being evenly distributed throughout the plumage without patchiness or dullness of tone. The various melanin mutations vary considerably in their appearance, in some the dilution and dispersal of the pigmentation being so complete as to make the bird appear almost as a clear! In those where the melanin pigment should be visible, it should be quite distinct upon the head, back and flanks of the bird, the pencilling being wide and of a deep colouring in some mutations but extremely fine and faint in others. All of these are detailed in the standards that follow at the end of the chapter.

tensive" in this case — should be entirely free from any frosting whatsoever. It has shown an unfortunate tendency to linger, however, but should be kept to an absolute minimum for it is considered a very bad fault for a large amount of frosting to be present around the neck and on the back. In the frosted birds, of course, the frosting

5.1   The Standard type for Coloured Canaries (as issued by the Canary Colour Breeders Association)

should be finely and evenly distributed all over the plumage with no tendency for it to be too heavy upon the back. With coloured canaries there is also an additional mutation known as **dimorphism** in which the coloured areas are differently distributed in cocks and hens and the description of these is included in the specialist society's standard later in this chapter.

EXHIBITING COLOURED CANARIES

Birds in this section of the fancy perhaps show a slight tendency towards being restless and flighty and so possibly the most important preparation for a fancier to make is to have his exhibition birds completely steady so that they will keep reasonably still while being examined by the judge instead of dashing about the cage. As with all show birds, however, this does not mean having them "frozen", or cowed, but confident, yet tame, and moving quite freely from perch to perch as a Border might do. They are not required to exhibit any special stance, or posture, and so the exhibitor has no extra training problems on that score. The usual proviso concerning immaculate presentation applies here; in fact, the specialist society's ruling states that a judge can deduct up to 20 points from any exhibit that is staged in a dirty, or non-standard, cage.

A detailed plan of this cage is published by the Canary Colour Breeders Association and is here reproduced with their permission.

OFFICIAL STANDARDS

1. **Points**

    Clears:

Lipochrome Colouring	50
Degree of Frosting	10
Type	30
Condition and Feather Quality	10
	100

    Selfs:

Lipochrome Colouring	25
Melanistic Colouring	25
Degree of Frosting	10
Type	30
Condition and Feather Quality	10
	100

A total of up to twenty points can be deducted by the judge from an exhibit staged in a dirty or non-standard cage.

2. **Specific Standards**
   1. The pictorial model will apply.
   2. The ideal length of a coloured canary is 5 inches.
   3. Lipochrome Colouring:
      (a) **RED** Colour to be a bright fiery red evenly distributed throughout the plumage.
      (b) **ROSE** to be a bright deep rich pink evenly distributed throughout the plumage.
      (c) **GOLD** colour to be of a bright yellow showing maximum optical blue.
         Faults: tendency of colour to be orangy yellow.
      (d) **DOMINANT WHITE.** Good clean white.
         Faults: Red or Yellow lipochrome appearing in the plumage.
      (e) **RECESSIVE WHITE.** As the action of this mutation is completely to mask all other traces of lipochrome colouring, nothing can be done either to improve or alternatively to cause a deterioration.
      (f) **IVORY WHITE.** Good clean white.
         Faults: whilst the ivory factor will normally mask the Yellow lipochrome often seen in the flight feathers of dominant white birds, it does tend to accentuate any Red or Yellow lipochrome present in the body feathers.
      (g) **IVORY GOLD.** A pleasant lemon yellow colouring showing maximum optical blue.
         Faults: tendency towards an orange-yellow colour.

3. **General faults covering all ground colours**
   Uneven depth and distribution of colour
   Dullness in colour.

4. **Melanistic Colouring**
   Where applicable, i.e. where melanin pigment should be present, melanins to be distinct over the head, back and flanks, progressing round into the chest area. Optical blue (reduction of brown) factor to be present.
   Faults:
      (a) Pencilling too coarse or faint and/or missing from flanks.
      (b) Light coloured feet, legs and beak in mutations where dark colouration is called for. Alternatively, dark coloured horny areas where light colouration is called for. (These are covered under general standards for the various mutations later in this text.)
      (c) The light area local to the vent must be to kept to a minimum with the obvious exception of dimorphics.
      (d) No foul birds or areas of variegation to be allowed in self birds. A bird with such faults to be immediately disqualified.

5. **Degrees of Frosting**
   (a) *Non-frosted.* All birds, ideally, should show no frosting whatever, but when this is present, it must be kept to an absolute minimum.
      Faults: too much frosting particularly round the neck and on the back.

(b) *Frosted.* Clear distinct frosting should be present and evenly distributed over the whole plumage.

Faults: irregular distribution of frosting often seen as either a frost free chest or a heavily frosted neck and back.

(c) *Dimporphic.* All must show the requirements of dimorphism, i.e. only four colour points; face, shoulders, rump and chest. To be more specific, these areas are itemised further:

Face: Hens to show "eyebrows" only. Colour not to run from eye to eye nor down to cheeks.

Cocks to show a blaze typical of a goldfinch, i.e. an area of colouration extending centrally from the beak and should be as restricted as possible.

Shoulders: Small distinct area on shoulders only. Colour not to extend to wing flights.

Rump: Small distinct area on top of rump, not to extend to back or under body.

Chest: Slight area centrally on chest, not to flow up or down to head or under body.

Remainder of body plumage, wings and tail to show bright clean white in clear varieties with corresponding colouring in self varieties.

The colour points of the cocks will be enlarged in comparison to hens.

Faults: (Hens particularly)

(a) Colouring above beak, on forehead, between beak and breast, running into wing flights.

(b) Rough feathering.

6. Feather Quality and Condition

Plumage to be close and firm in texture, presenting a smooth silky appearance giving a clear cut contour to body. The bird to be in full bloom of perfect health, clean, jaunty, bouncing in a steady manner.

7. Type

(a) *Body outline.* Short and full to conform with agreed outline. Back well filled in showing a slight rise transversely. Chest broad and full, giving a nicely rounded front at an angle of 45 degrees approximately to perch.

(b) *Head.* A full forehead rising from a short neat beak, to be well rounded over and across skull. Eyes distinct, clear and bright.

(c) *Neck.* Short and distinct, flowing neatly from back skull on to shoulders and from a full throat into breast.

(d) *Wings.* Short and well braced meeting nicely at tips to rest lightly, yet closely, on rump. (Tips of wings to end on rump.) Flights to rest together, neatly tapering off gradually along wings.

(e) *Tail.* Complete, short and tightly packed, well filled in at root. To be carried rigidly, giving an all in line appearance to the body.

(f) *Legs and Feet.* Legs well set back, free from scale, feet perfect, all nails showing.

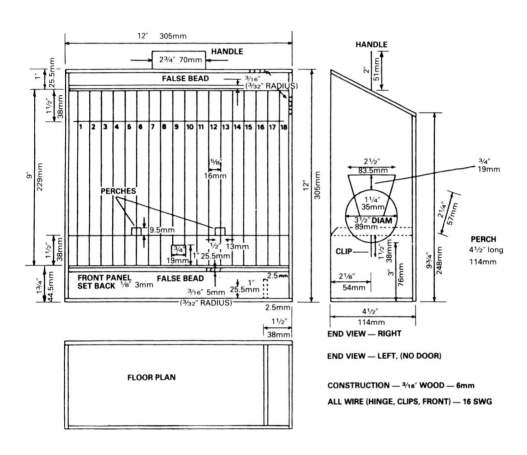

5.2 Details of Show Cage used for all Coloured Canaries

8. **Individual Standards**

Clears.

All birds regardless of ground colour must comply with the specific standard relating to lipochrome colour, degree of frosting, etc.

Variegation is permitted in all varieties with the exception of the dimorphic where birds showing melanistic pigment in excess of one tick mark must be disqualified. Variegation is defined as follows:

> *Clear:*   A bird showing no melanistic pigmentation in its plumage whatever.
>
> *Ticked:*   A bird with one dark mark in its plumage coverable by a one penny piece.
>
> *Variegated:* A bird having either more than one tick mark or melanistic pigment in excess of that coverable by a one penny piece, up to a self bird with one foul feather.
>
> **N.B.** 1. Dark colouration on the horny areas must be discounted.
>   2. In all classes where a clear bird is considered equal in all areas to a ticked or variegated bird, the clear will take preference.

Selfs.

All varieties must conform with the specific standards regarding lipochrome colour, degree of frosting, etc., as well as the specific rule for all self varieties. Individual varieties should conform to the following rules:

Brown and Green to show maximum deep coloured wide pencilling which should be distinct. Optical blue factor giving a reduction of phaeomelanin brown. Green birds to show jet black horny areas. Brown birds to have flesh coloured horny areas.

Isabel and Agate. The same standard as for Brown and Green except that the pencilling should be extremely fine. The horny areas in both instances to be flesh coloured.

Brown Pastel. Distinct but fine pencilling with an overlaying brown suffusion. Flesh coloured horny areas.

Isabel Pastel. Pencilling absent, brown suffusion present but diluted.

Green Pastel. Pencilling to be broad but distinct and of a dark grey colour except in the wings and tail where a broad pale silvery grey bar flanked with a narrower bar of dark grey on either side should be visible, i.e. showing maximum grey wing effect. Horny areas to be dark with a black tip to the beak and each claw.

Agate Pastel. Pencilling to be as fine as possible and of a dark grey colour. Horny areas flesh coloured.

Brown Satinette. Maxium brown pencilling. Flesh coloured horny areas.

Isabel Satinette. As with the brown satinette but with the pencilling finer.

Agate and Green Satinette. Extremely fine brown pencilling. Flesh coloured horny areas.

Green Opal. Pencilling to be distinct and broad of a silvery grey colour. Horny areas to be jet black.

Agate Opal. As with the green opal, but pencilling to be finer and horny areas flesh coloured.

Brown and Green Ino. Pencilling to be broad and distinct with phaeomelanin on feather tips expressed to the maximum. Horny areas flesh coloured.

Isabel and Agate Ino. Standards as for the green and brown ino except that all melanin will be finer and less distinct.

SHOW RULES

1. **Standard Show Cage**
   1. All exhibits to be shown in the standard Colour Canary Show Cage (specification opposite) of the correct colours.*
   2. Colours to be: Interior — Dulux Summer Blue
                     Exterior — Black Gloss
   3. Cage fronts may be secured by pins as shown or preferably by the extension of the fourth wire from each end.
   4. Floor covering should be of a mixed seed, i.e. that which the exhibit is usually fed in the bird-room.
   5. A small size black 'D' shape drinker is to be used.
2. **Novice Rule**
   A novice may retain this status for six years from the date of joining the CCBA provided that he/she has not previously shown as a Champion in another section of the canary fancy. At any time, an exhibitor may take Champion status, but will not be allowed to return to Novice status after doing so.

In Britain, coloured canaries are catered for by the Canary Colour Breeders Association whose origins lay as far back as 1935 in the Red Canary Movement. To broaden the basis and cover *all* the developments in coloured canaries this was superseded by the Canary Colour Research Association in 1938. After the second world war the society was reorganised under the present title and, so popular have coloured canaries become, that there are now a number of regional zones, each autonomous yet still responsible to the parent body whose standards have been given above.

*It has recently (1984) been decided to adopt the show cage of the Red Canary Association. A period of ten years is to be allowed for the changeover in order to accommodate those fanciers who still possess cages of the original pattern.

6.0   Yellow Variegated Dutch Crest (around 1900)

Chapter 6

THE CRESTED

HISTORY

The Crested Canary is a very ancient, and one-time favourite, breed that was originally known to fanciers as the **Turn-crown** or **Turncrest.** The head adornment that is
so characteristic of the variety is a mutant form that appeared sometime during the
eighteenth century, presumably between 1713, when it went unmentioned in Hervieux' latest list of canary varieties, and 1793 when it was added to that list in Buffon's
Histoire Naturelle.

Such an unusual feature as a crest clearly made an appeal to the breeders of the day
for, by the middle of the nineteenth century, there were crested forms to be found in
several of the then-popular breeds such as the Norwich, Lancashire and Belgian, as
well as among ordinary common canaries and German Rollers too. In some of these it
has persisted as an established feature to this day but in others it has disappeared.

In Britain the Crest had achieved a great following by mid-Victorian times when
large numbers of fanciers who bred the highly popular Norwich canary also seem to
have incorporated the crested form in their stocks. Thus, there existed side by side the
Norwich **Plainhead** and the Norwich **Crested** which the illustrations in old canary
books depicted to be identical, apart from the presence or absence of the crest on the
bird's head.

As explained in the chapter on Standards, the ideals of fanciers do not remain static
and, in efforts to improve the size and development of the crest, they were severely limited within the Norwich breed itself where great emphasis was placed upon colour
and feather quality. New blood was therefore sought by the introduction of the Lancashire Coppy (crested) Canary which was a very large bird, around 8 inches in
length, rather coarse in feather quality, but with a vastly better development of the
crest which radiated well over the beak and eyes.

The first examples of this outcross are recorded as having been exhibited in 1879
when they were rejected by the judges as not being true examples of the Crested Norwich. Nevertheless it was clear to many that the crest itself had been substantially improved in these birds although the bodily conformation was now quite different from
that which was approved by the Norwich Plainhead men. It was not long, however,
before many more birds of the new type were being shown, and eventually accepted
by the fancy, as the older Norwich Crested Canary was ousted from the showbench.
The "new" birds, in fact, had the name of Norwich dropped from their title and became known simply as Crested Canaries, although old habits die hard in the canary
fancy and many people still persist in calling them Crested Norwich to this day. (Such
are the vagaries of fashion, however, that subsequent developments in the Norwich

Canary itself have brought the two breeds much closer in appearance once again — but that story belongs to the chapter on the Norwich!)

In its heyday, the Crested Canary had a tremendous following and became one of the leading exhibition varieties. Such was the craze for them that some of the highest prices ever paid in the canary fancy, at comparable rates, were acknowledged to have been given for outstanding birds. Unfortunately, this was to have its effect by forcing many less well-to-do fanciers out of the hobby and, over the years, the Crest started to lose ground.

This decline has continued right down to the present day so that the Crested Canary is now only a minority breed in the hands of relatively few fanciers. Fortunately, there are always some who are prepared to persevere with the minority varieties, however, and at the present time there are clear signs that the Crest has passed its lowest ebb, and more are now appearing on the showbench than at any time in the past fifty years.

POINTS OF THE CRESTED CANARY

In all crested varieties of the canary there are two types of bird that constitute the breed as a whole, namely, those which actually possess a crest and those that do not. The reason for this lies in the genetical implications of the crested gene which, if present in a double "dose" (i.e. on both chromosomes), has a lethal effect and renders the individual unable to survive after hatching. (Full explanations of the breeding procedures with crested breeds are usually included in the better canary textbooks and so are not repeated here in a book primarily concerned with exhibiting). Nomenclature varies from breed to breed but in this case the crested birds are, quite rationally, called "Crests" and the plain-headed birds are known as "Crest-breds".

Apart from the obvious difference in the head properties of these two forms, the bodily conformation, or basic type, is exactly the same which, in general appearance, should be something like that of the bullfinch. The bird should have a bold head, a short and thickset neck, and a body that is broad across the back and deep through the chest. It stands at a fairly low angle across the perch and has shortish legs, well set back, and with strong feet and claws. The general length of feather possessed by Crested Canaries tends to produce wings and tail that are on the long side also, although the standard encourages them to be kept as compact as possible and, as with most other breeds, they should be closely folded.

In this breed, of course, it is the crest itself that is by far the most important single feature and it is often said that a judge need look at nothing else! (Broadly speaking this is true, and it is only when two exhibits of absolutely equal merit as regards their crests need to be separated that he will resort to other distinguishing features). The crest can never be too large in size and should be circular in shape when viewed from above. In the heyday of the breed the standard object for comparison was the old-fashioned five shilling piece but it is doubtful whether any but the very best would have measured up to this. The crest is composed of a radiating circlet of feathers from a small centre on the top of the head and it should be composed of a profusion of broad, long feathers that fall evenly over the beak, eyes and back of the head. If the feathers are too short, they tend to produce a flat crest which, although tolerated, will always be inferior to the larger, drooping form.

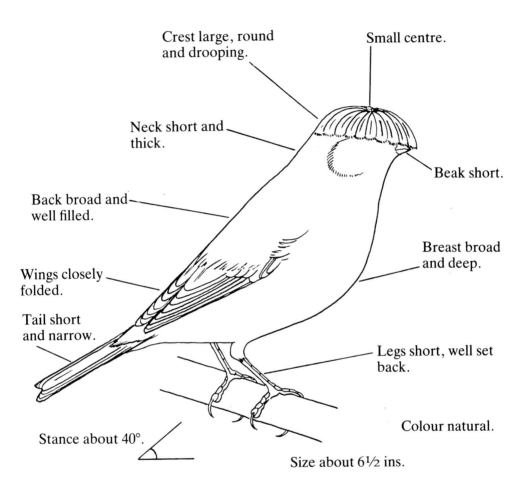

Crest large, round and drooping.

Small centre.

Neck short and thick.

Beak short.

Back broad and well filled.

Breast broad and deep.

Wings closely folded.

Tail short and narrow.

Legs short, well set back.

Stance about 40°.

Colour natural.

Size about 6½ ins.

6.1   The Points of a Crested Canary

In such a spectacular feature as the crest, exhibition faults naturally tend to be numerous. Firstly, there are defects in **shape** when the crest, instead of being circular, may be somewhat elongated into an oval, or broader at one end giving it an ovate form. Sometimes it may be so pinched at the front that the crest takes on a shield shape or, in bad cases, even almost triangular. Needless to say, such departures from the ideal circular form, are at a grave disadvantage on the show bench although they are not actually listed as disqualifications. Secondly, there are faults in the **position** of the crest which may be off-centre to some extent, thus causing it to be tilted in one direction or another, either forwards, backwards or to one side, giving the bird a very unbalanced effect.

Thirdly, there may be defects in the **feathering** of the crest which, as mentioned in an earlier paragraph, should be well filled in and radiate evenly all round from a small, neat centre. This centre should be clearly discernible but should not suggest anything resembling a bald spot. The crest feathers should then lie neatly and in a regular fashion all round like the spokes of a wheel with neither split nor break at any point of the circle. Other faults may occur in the form of unruly tufts, or "horns", of feathers sticking up out of place which clearly would break up the desired evenness of the outline. Finally, the feathers should always be broad and leafy in shape, and never thin and hairy.

Turning to the other half of the breed, the Crest-breds, they also should have a head that is covered with an abundance of long, broad, feathering although they will not, in this case, take on the formation of the crest so far described. Instead, starting from the base of the upper mandible, the feathers will sweep over the crown of the head in the usual way but, being of such a length, if turned over with a pencil, they will reach the tip of the beak, or even beyond it. Because of this length, the head feathers of the Crest-bred tend to hang over the eyes, often obscuring them and producing a somewhat frowning, or sulky appearance, a good point in an exhibition bird.

Today, owing to lack of numbers, Crested Canaries are rarely accorded a full classification on the showbench although, in the past, special provision was made for those beautiful examples of the breeder's art — the clear bodied birds with a dark crest and, perhaps even more attractive, clear bodied birds possessing not only a dark crest but evenly marked wings also. It must be appreciated, however, that markings in themselves, no matter how attractive, have no particular advantage and a heavily variegated, or self green bird of superior type would always take preference over a perfectly marked, yet inferior, specimen.

EXHIBITING THE CRESTED CANARY

Not being of a highly-strung or nervous disposition, nor being required to show off any particular position or jaunty carriage, the Crested Canary poses no great problem for the exhibitor. The usual basic preparation, common to all exhibition canary breeds, should be heeded, however, so that the bird is put down in a clean and immaculate condition and be well accustomed to having its cage handled by the judge. Because of their long feathering in the region of the vent, Crested Canaries sometimes tend to be somewhat dirty in this area and so naturally careful attention should be paid to this before sending them out to a show.

The importance of the bird's main feature, the crest itself, cannot be over-emphasised and the keen exhibitor will often spend a lot of time on grooming it so that it will lay down well and radiate evenly all round in the approved manner. This can be done by gently brushing it daily with a very soft brush, such as a shaving brush or baby's toothbrush, that has been dipped in warm water. It must be appreciated, however, that it is impossible to turn a bad crest into a good one in this way — only that *some* improvements can be made. If a bird has been bred with naturally unruly tufts, horns or splits they can never be eradicated merely by grooming, although it is not unethical to remove the odd errant feather with tweezers. Too free a use of this article, however, would be frowned upon and in any case, would easily be detected by the judge.

The show cage for Crests and Crest-breds is of a "box" pattern, that is to say it is all made of wood with the exception of the wire front. It is 12ins wide, 10ins high and 5¼ins deep, with a circular door 3½ins in diameter at the right-hand end. It is painted black on the outside and eau-de-nil inside. The wire front has the wires more widely spaced than those for most other breeds of canary, ¾in. instead of the more usual ½in. or ⅝in., and the drinker hole is also a good deal larger (1½ins. diameter) in order to minimise damage to the crest as the bird puts its head through to drink. The top part of the wire front curves backwards so that the judge can obtain a good view of the crest from above. The standard two-hook 'D' shaped show cage drinker, either in metal or plastic, is used and the floor of the cage should be covered with seed when the bird is sent out to a show.

OFFICIAL STANDARD

There is no "Scale of Points" attached to the standard of the Crested Canary, merely a written description which is as follows: —

"Size and formation of the crest shall be the first consideration. A crest cannot be too large. It should consist of an abundance of broad, long and veiny feathers, evenly radiated from a small centre, well over eyes, beak and poll. A good crest may be flat if well filled in at the back and without splits, but a drooping or weeping crest shall have preference. Type and quality are of next importance. The body should in shape resemble that of the bullfinch possessing substance in proportion to its length, with a broad back, nicely arched, full and well circled chest, tail short and narrow, wings not extending beyond the root of the tail, nor crossed at the tips, but fitting closely to the body. The neck should be full and the beak short. The bird should stand well across the perch on short legs, with thighs and hocks well set back. The Crest-bred should possess a body as above described. The head should be large and round, broad at every part, with a small beak and abundance of long, broad feather commencing at entrance of beak, continuing over the crown, and flowing well down the poll and should be well browed. In a good Crest-bred the feathers of the crown when turned over should reach the end of the beak and the heavy brows should give the bird a sulky appearance without brushing. When two or more birds are of equal merit in crest or head properties the smaller bird shall take precedence if of the correct type, the Club recognising it to be the more difficult to obtain, but

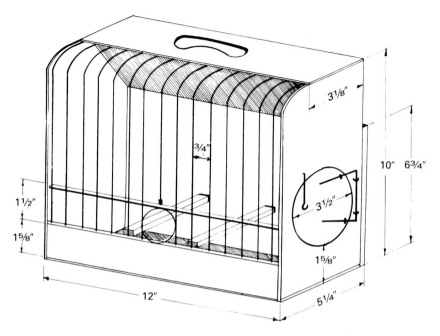

6.2   Crest & Crest Bred Show Cage

no restriction whatever is placed on the length of the bird. Quality of feather and high condition to have due weight.

"**Objectionable Properties** — (1) Crest and Head. Crests shall not be horned at back, nor open at poll, nor split at sides or front; nor shall the centre be open or long, or too near the beak, back or sides; nor shall the crest be tilted, nor shall it consist of thin, scanty, hairy feather. The head of a Crest-bred shall not be narrow in any part, nor pinched over beak, nor should it be flat or covered with short, scanty feather, or be rough or "guttered". (2) Body. Crests and Crest-breds should not have long, thin, erect bodies with disproportionately long tails, should not be dipped in back or frilled on breast, or cross their wings at tips, or carry themselves in a curved or slovenly manner, or stand on long legs, and no show bird should possess such an amount of loose fluff or body feather as to make it difficult to make out its shape."

There is one specialist society for this breed in Great Britain, the Crested Canary Club, although the Old Varieties Canary Association also makes provision for it along with the other ancient varieties under its care.

Chapter 7

THE NORTH DUTCH FRILL

In the same way that a distinct mutation gave rise to the Crested Canary and the other crested breeds still to be dealt with, so yet another form affecting the disposition of the feathering was the foundation material for several other varieties, all of Continental origin. This was the **frilled** mutation which, since its appearance, has been developed into a number of specific breeds which differ from one another in matters of detail concerning size and posture, and in the extent to which their frilled feathering has been developed.

As far as can be ascertained, this mutation occurred in Holland about the year 1800, allegedly among a stock of the so-called "Old Dutch" canary previously referred to in the chapter on the Belgian. Coming at a time when "fancying" was beginning to develop as a hobby, such a highly ornamental feature as frilled plumage was certain to be the object of attention, particularly with the view to perfecting it as an exhibition form according to the ideals that were prevalent at that time. Birds possessing the frilled characteristic were all originally called simply Dutch canaries, but, as the type spread to various other countries where canary fancying was practised, local breeders, working with the material they had at hand, began to produce their own versions which finally led to the establishment of several distinctive breeds.

Some of these have subsequently become extinct, others have been absorbed in the making of new varieties, but several of the older ones fortunately have survived to the present day. Of the latter, the North Dutch Frill is not only the oldest of all frilled breeds, but also must be regarded as the "classic" example of its kind in which all of the frills should be displayed to perfection.

POINTS OF THE NORTH DUTCH FRILL

Just as a canary's crest consists of feathers disposed in a certain basic arrangement (i.e. radiating in a circle from a central point on the crown of the head) so it is with the curled feathers of the frilled mutation. In this case, however, there are *three* areas of the body where the frills are to be found, each frill being known by a distinctive name.

First, there is the **mantle** which is formed by the feathers on the back being divided by a central parting and curling forwards like a cape over each shoulder. Secondly, there is the **breast** where the feathers form a kind of frilly "shirt front" by curling forwards and inwards towards the centre. Finally there are the **flanks** where bunches of feathers rising from just above the thighs sweep upwards and outwards around the wings. All of the frilled varieties of canary possess this fundamental feather pattern and any further frilling, or lack of it, plus the size and posture of the bird, distinguishes between the various breeds.

The North Dutch Frill, in fact, should have these three basic frills *only,* with no other curled feathering appearing anywhere else about the body. It is a medium to large sized bird of about 17 to 18 cm. in length, and stands erect, well up on longish legs, showing plenty of nerve and alertness and with the head, body and tail in line. The plumage should be soft and abundant, with the frills well developed and showing up clearly with complete symmetry, and giving to the bird a well-groomed appearance like a freshly-set "perm". Any roughness or wayward feathering should be avoided, for it is the exactitude and correctness of formation that is all important.

As stated above, the three basic frills only should be present, with the head, neck, rump, abdomen and thighs being smoothly feathered without any trace of curling whatsoever. All of the usual canary colour forms are permissible so that the North Dutch Frill may appear on the showbench as a clear, ticked, marked, variegated, foul or self bird, either in green or cinnamon, or on a yellow or white background.

EXHIBITING THE NORTH DUTCH FRILL

All frilled canaries tend to be rather highly strung and with a somewhat nervous manner. This is quite correct and they should display their "nerve" when in the showcage by standing up well and being alert and lively. As so often happens with highly-bred livestock possessing this kind of temperament, however, they may be "triggered off" by some distraction or other and become wild and flutter about the cage and so, perhaps, the most important thing for any exhibitor to do is to have his birds tame and steady. The same kind of training as that recommended for the Belgian will be found to be most effective except that no additional work is necessary to produce any special posture; the bird should merely by required to stand erect upon its perch with an intelligent alertness while it is being judged.

Care of the precious frills might be thought to present a difficult problem and yet, if kept under conditions of scrupulous cleanliness, they should cause little trouble. If the birds are allowed the regular use of their bath they will keep themselves in a nice, hard condition with the frills all cripsly curled but it is a curious feature of birds of the frilled breeds that, if they are a bit out of condition, the frills begin to lose their curl and a bird that is really unwell may temporarily lose its frills altogether. For success on the showbench, therefore, it is clearly important to send out only birds that are really bouncing with health so that their frills will appear at their very best.

In Britain all of the frilled breeds can be shown in exactly the same type and size of show cage as is the Belgian which is helpful to any fancier who is attracted to these various continental varieties as he is spared the expense and inconvenience of having a large stock of different patterns of show cage. To save repetition, reference should be made to the chapter on the Belgian and a working diagram of the showcage is also given.

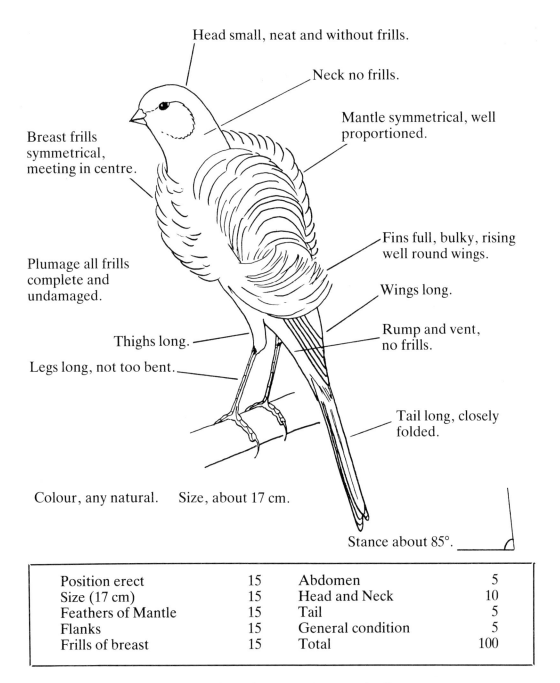

Head small, neat and without frills.

Neck no frills.

Mantle symmetrical, well proportioned.

Breast frills symmetrical, meeting in centre.

Plumage all frills complete and undamaged.

Fins full, bulky, rising well round wings.

Wings long.

Thighs long.

Legs long, not too bent.

Rump and vent, no frills.

Tail long, closely folded.

Colour, any natural.   Size, about 17 cm.

Stance about 85°.

Position erect	15	Abdomen	5
Size (17 cm)	15	Head and Neck	10
Feathers of Mantle	15	Tail	5
Flanks	15	General condition	5
Frills of breast	15	Total	100

7.1   The Points of a North Dutch Frill Canary

OFFICIAL STANDARDS

In Britain the original standard for the North Dutch Frill was adopted as follows: —

	points
Head and Neck: Small, neat and without any frills.	15
Mantle: Symmetrical and well proportioned. No additional frilling.	15
Breast: Frills symmetrical, complete and well filled.	15
Flanks: Full, bulky and even, rising towards the shoulders.	15
Legs and Feet: Long thighs, normally feathered, legs not too bent.	10
Plumage: Frills complete and undamaged, symmetrical.	10
Size: Length 17 to 18 cm. Perfectly proportioned.	10
Condition: Healthy, clean and entire.	10
	100

Since then, the **Confederation Ornithologique Mondiale** has amended, reworded and made slight adjustments to the points as follow:

1. **Neck:** clearly visible, no frilling.
2. **Mantle:** symmetrical, well proportioned without additional frilling.
3. **Wings:** long, lying close to the body.
4. **Tail:** long, narrow, in straight line with back.
5. **Head:** small, neat, no frills.
6. **Beak:** fine.
7. **Breast:** frills symmetrical and complete.
8. **Flanks:** full, bulky, rising toward shoulders.
9. **Under Body:** free from frilling.
10. **Legs:** long, not too bent, normal feathering.
    Position: slightly bent, but standing well 85°.
    Plumage: frills undamaged and symmetrical.
    Size: 17 cm.

Points allocated by the COM are shown in Fig. 7.1.

The North Dutch Frill is catered for in Britain by the **Old Varieties Canary Association.**

Plate 1

Belgian Canary in full Show Position

Plate 2

Border Fancy Canary

Plate 3

Border Fancy Canaries – Ticked Buff and Variegated Yellow

Plate 4

Coloured Canaries (Selfs) –
Gold Brown Satinette (above)
Silver Agate Opal and Red Orange Isabel (below)

Plate 5

Coloured Canaries (Clears) – Rose and Ivory Pastel

Plate 6

Crested Canaries –
Dark Crested Wing Marked Crest
and Variegated Crestbred

Plate 7

Crested Canaries –

Clear Bodied Dark Crest and Self Green Crestbred

Plate 8

North Dutch Frilled Canary

Plate 9

South Dutch Frilled Canary

Plate 10

Fife Fancy Canary

Plate 11

Fife Fancy Canaries — Self Green and Wing Marked Buff

Plate 12

Gibber Italicus Canary

Plate 13

Gibber Italicus Canaries – Two further views

Plate 14

Gloster Fancy Canaries – Clear Consort and Variegated Corona

Plate 15

Gloster Fancy Canaries – Clear Bodied Dark Corona and Self Green Consort

Plate 16

Lancashire Canaries – Coppy and Plainhead

Chapter 8

THE SOUTH DUTCH FRILL

Frilled canaries from the north of Holland soon spread to the southern Netherlands, later to become independent as modern Belgium, where they were incorporated with the **postuurvogel,** or Belgian canary, to produce the breed under discussion in the present chapter. This same type of bird was also bred across the border in French Flanders by the fanciers of Roubaix and Lille so that, as a result, the COM now recognises three alternative names for the breed; South Dutch Frill, Belgian Frill and French Frill. Of these, probably the most apt, descriptively, is the Belgian Frill since that is precisely what the bird is — a Belgian canary with frills. However, if the normal rules of nomenclature are followed, the first name given should be the correct one and so South Dutch Frill has been preferred in this book.

POINTS OF THE SOUTH DUTCH FRILL

As explained, this breed is the result of combining the frilled feather formation with the bodily characteristics and show position of the Belgian **postuurvogel** so that, in effect, we have a frilled Belgian canary. Much of what has been written in the previous chapters on the Belgian and the North Dutch Frill, therefore, is equally applicable to this variety and need not be repeated. The three basic frills only should be visible, as in the case of the North Dutch, but with the minor difference that they need not be quite so intensely developed, although still possessing the required perfection and symmetry of form. The size of the bird, as given by the COM, is again 17 cm. although this is, of course, only a guide as many birds would vary a centimetre or so either side of this. As in most breeds of canary, judges tend to give preference to a larger bird, all other things being equal, but here it is the posture plus the frills that are the main thing and size is quite a secondary consideration. In the show cage the South Dutch Frill should be capable of adopting the same typical "figure of seven" attitude as the Belgian in order to display both its posture, and its frills, to full advantage when handled by the judge.

EXHIBITING THE SOUTH DUTCH FRILL

There are no differences in exhibiting the South Dutch Frill and the two breeds that went into its make-up. Training methods and the type of show cage used in Britain are the same and so reference should be made to earlier chapters for the necessary details.

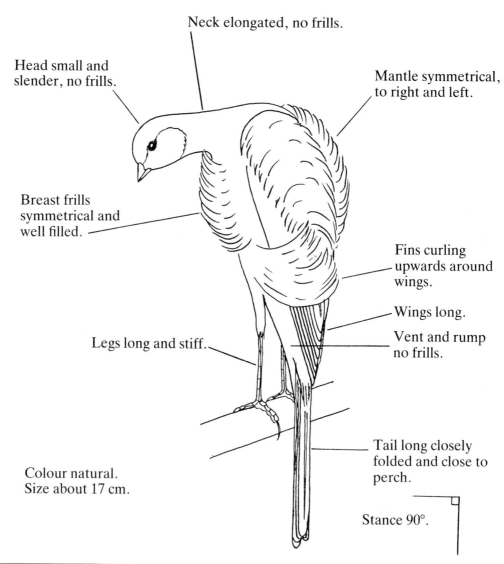

Neck elongated, no frills.

Head small and
slender, no frills.

Mantle symmetrical,
to right and left.

Breast frills
symmetrical and
well filled.

Fins curling
upwards around
wings.

Wings long.

Legs long and stiff.

Vent and rump
no frills.

Colour natural.
Size about 17 cm.

Tail long closely
folded and close to
perch.

Stance 90°.

Position and form	10	Legs — rigid carriage, thighs		
Size	10	featherd		15
Plumage	10	Tail		5
Shoulders	10	Wings		5
Jabot	10	Head		10
Fins	10	General Condition		5
		Total		100

(**N.B.** It will be noted that here the COM uses the term "Jabot" for the frills on the breast and "Fins" for those on the flanks. Both terms are also freely used in Britain.)

8.1   The Points of a South Dutch Frill Canary

OFFICIAL STANDARDS

As in the case of the North Dutch Frill, the original standard adopted by the Old Varieties Canary Association in Britain has since been amended and reworded by the Confederation Ornithologique Mondiale. Both versions are again given, although it should be realised that the ideal bird is **exactly the same** in both cases:

	points
Carriage: In the form of a figure seven, neck extended and square with the back.	15
Size: 16 to 17 cm.	5
Head and Neck: Small and slender, neck elongated.	15
Mantle: Curving symmetrically to left and right.	15
Breast: Forming a small "basket", well filled and perfect	15
Flanks: Curling upwards and well raised up.	15
Legs and Feet: Legs stiff, thighs not showing.	10
Tail: Long, closely folded and almost touching the perch	5
Condition: Healthy, clean and perfect.	5
	100

1. **Head:** small, slender, serpent like.
2. **Breast:** small but well filled "basket".
3. **Under Body:** sleek feathered.
4. **Flanks:** full, bulky, rising towards shoulder.
5. **Underflue:** smooth feathered.
6. **Legs:** straight.
7. **Neck:** elongated, slender.
8. **Mantle:** curving symmetrically to left and right.
9. **Back and Tail:** in straight line.
10. **Wings:** close to body.
11. **Feathering:** soft and undamaged.
12. **Tail:** long, closed, almost touching perch.
    Position: forming figure of seven (7). Neck extended and square with back.
    Size: 17 cm.

There are very few South Dutch Frills to be found in Britain at the present time as they are by no means plentiful even in their native country. Any fancier intending to exhibit them will find that they are catered for in the classification of the OVCA.

JUDGING "SCOTCH FANCY CANARY"—THREE SCOTTISH WORTHIES.

A judging session in Victorian times

Chapter 9

THE FIFE FANCY

A MINIATURE CANARY

Unlike the poultry fancy, where bantams are generally more popular as exhibition birds than the standard fowl, in the canary world the concept of miniature versions of the normal breeds has never been one to arouse much enthusiasm — probably because canaries are small enough creatures in any case. However, in the Fife Fancy, which is in effect a miniature form of the Border Fancy, we have a breed that, since its inception, has made enormous strides in popularity.

The origin of the Fife Fancy clearly lies in the Border itself which, it will be recalled, was affectionately known in the fancy as "wee gem" in the early days of its history. Since the second world war, however, there has been a considerable increase in the size of the Border, many of them now being almost the equal of some Norwich, so that the old epithet "wee" is clearly inappropriate.

It is therefore probable that the Fife Fancy arose as a direct result of the dissatisfaction that was felt by some Border breeders at this increase in size so that those who have wished to continue with their "wee gems", and keep them really tiny, have been able to do so through the medium of the Fife. Whatever the basic reason for its origin, the canary fancy now has in its midst a really charming little bird that is not much larger than a blue tit.

The specialist society that fosters the breeding and exhibiting of these little birds was formed at Kirkaldy in 1957 and, at first, interest and progress was relatively slow but, in the past 10 years or so, Fifes have gained a tremendous following and have their devotees not only in Scotland, but all over the British Isles as well. There is even a **South of England Fife Fancy Canary Club** among the specialist societies today and the breed has also been taken up on the continent and the U.S.A.

POINTS OF THE FIFE FANCY

Since the Fife is virtually a miniature Border, most of what has already been written about that breed is equally applicable to the Fife with the sole exception, of course, of its size. In general terms it is a neat, active, nicely rounded little bird that has a most confiding manner as it bounces buoyantly from perch to perch. This freedom of action is an essential of a good show specimen just as in the Border and certain other breeds and a bird that is lethargic and unwilling to move is the very antithesis of what a Fife Fancy should be.

As to the detailed make-up of the breed, starting with the head, this should be as round as a marble with no flatness on the crown or above the beak. It should be relatively small, with a fine beak and with the eye bright and alert and centrally placed.

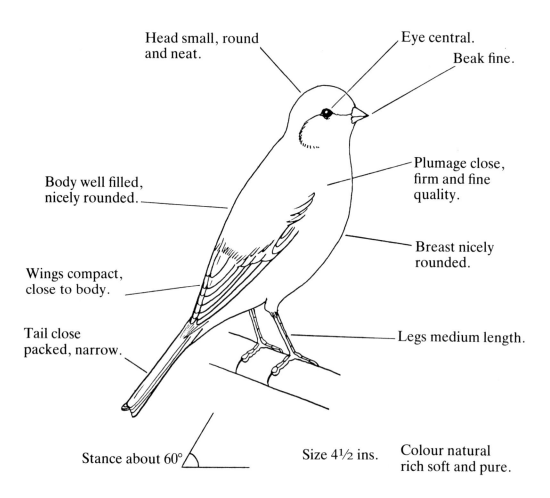

Head small, round and neat.

Eye central.

Beak fine.

Plumage close, firm and fine quality.

Body well filled, nicely rounded.

Breast nicely rounded.

Wings compact, close to body.

Tail close packed, narrow.

Legs medium length.

Stance about 60°

Size 4½ ins.

Colour natural rich soft and pure.

9.1   The Points of a Fife Fancy Canary

The body should give the impression of a nicely rounded bird with every feature in balance, the feathering being close, firm and of exceptionally fine quality. From a neck of moderate length, the back should rise gently over the shoulders and then taper gradually away to the base of the tail. From beneath the throat, the breast and underparts, too, should be nicely rounded in one continuous curve but should not be too prominent or deep-chested. Some Fifes, indeed, do tend to be a bit "full" here but, although the standard states that the chest should not be too heavy or prominent, this is perhaps preferable to the bird being too slim and tapering in this feature.

The wings and tail in this breed should be very compact and on the short side. The wings should be closely folded, with the tips of the flight feathers meeting but not overlapping, and ending just below the root of the tail. The tail itself should be carried in a line with the rest of the body and consist of closely packed feathers so that it is quite narrow and pencil slim, or "piped" to use an old fanciers' expression. It should never have the appearance of being spread, broad or coarse.

The bearing of the Fife, as has already been stated, should be sprightly and confident, with a bold, bright eye and a jaunty carriage of the head. The position of the body should be semi-erect at an angle of about 60 degrees, borne upon legs of medium length which show little, if any, of the thigh joint.

The colour should be pure, soft and level throughout the body and in natural colour only, no colour feeding being allowed. The full range of markings are permitted, both in green and cinnamon, and white ground birds are found as well as the normal yellow ground colour.

The diminutive size of the Fife has already been emphasised and the bird should not, in fact, exceed 4¼ inches which is really quite small when compared with the giants of the canary fancy such as the Lancashire and the Parisian Frill which can run to almost twice that length.

EXHIBITING THE FIFE FANCY

This breed needs the usual basic training common to all varieties of canary, starting in the early post-weaning weeks by hanging a show cage on the front of the stock cage to allow the young birds to become accustomed to it. After teaching them to run into the show cage on command, this progresses to handling the cage freely so that the trainee is not flustered by this kind of treatment — not usually a difficult task with Fifes owing to their natural tameness.

As with the Border, the final stages of their training should consist of encouraging the birds to stand in the approved posture in order to show themselves off to advantage and then to move freely and lightly from perch to perch when required to do so.

Up to the time of writing, Fifes have been shown in the original "Dewar" cage that is used for Borders but a new cage is at present under consideration and may possibly be adopted before this book appears in print. It is based upon the Dewar pattern but is smaller and has other minor modifications including a different type of drinker and the positioning of the drinker hole plus the abandonment of oat husks as a floor covering in favour of seed. In order to cover all eventualities details of both cages are here included but exhibitors should wait until the new cage has been officially adopted before making any alterations.

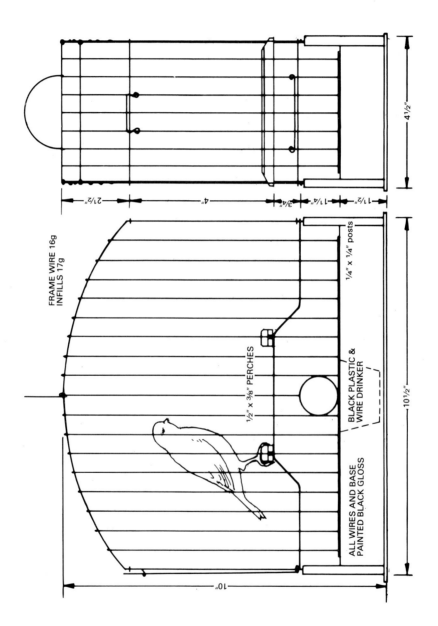

FRAME WIRE 16g
INFILLS 17g

2½"

4"

¾"

1¼"

1½"

4½"

½" × ⅜" PERCHES

BLACK PLASTIC &
WIRE DRINKER

¼" × ¼" posts

ALL WIRES AND BASE
PAINTED BLACK GLOSS

10½"

10"

9.2 Proposed New Show Cage for Fife Fancies — at present unrecognised.

9.3   Fife Fancy Canary
Official drawing issued by the Fife Fancy Canary Club

The Dewar cage, it will be recalled, is of an open wire pattern with the exception of the wooden base and corner posts and is painted entirely black. It is rectangular in shape with the base being 12¼ inches long and 4½ inches wide. The height is 9¼ inches at the sides, rising to 11¼ inches at the top of the arched top. At the left hand side there is a three-wired sliding door and, at the opposite end a seed trough is provided at floor level; this is partially covered but has a slot in it to allow the bird access to the seed. The perches are ½ inch in diameter and are what is known as "spirally turned" with 12 spirals, and no other pattern of perch is permitted at shows governed by the specialist societies. These perches should be so placed as to leave five empty wires between them.

Small sized show cage drinkers only should be used and are attached opposite to the left hand perch. As with Borders, the specified floor covering is that of oat husks, and the cage labels containing the class numbers must be affixed directly under the perch opposite to the drinker, i.e. the right hand perch. Any subsequent award labels should be placed immediately to the left of the class label.

The Fife specialist clubs are particularly insistent upon accurate compliance with their show cage specifications and any failure to observe seemingly minor points may debar members from competing for their specials. Thus it is in the interests of exhibitors to ensure that every detail is correct by checking with the society's rule book.

OFFICIAL STANDARD

The Official Standard and Scale of Points for the Fife Fancy reads as follows:
Points
10 **Head:** Small round and neat — beak fine; eyes central to roundness of head and body.
10 **Body:** Well filled and nicely rounded running in almost a straight line from the gentle rise over the shoulders to the point of the tail, chest also rounded, but neither heavy nor prominent.
10 **Wings:** Compact and carried close to the body, meeting at the tips, just below root of tail.
 5 **Legs:** Of medium length, showing little thigh.
10 **Plumage:** Close, firm, fine in quality.
 5 **Tail:** Close packed and narrow being nicely founded and filled in at the root.
10 **Position & Carriage:** Semi-erect, standing at an angle of 60°. Gay, jaunty, with full poise of head.
10 **Colour:** Rich, soft and pure, as level in tint as possible throughout, but extreme depth and hardness such as colour feeding gives are **debarred.**
 5 **Health:** Condition and cleanliness shall have due weight.
25 **Size:** Not to exceed **4¼ inches.**

The original specialist society, based in Scotland, is the Fife Fancy Canary Club but further societies promoting this breed are tending to spring up, mostly of a regional nature as, for example, the South of England Fife Fancy Canary Club.

Chapter 10

THE GIBBER ITALICUS

ORIGINS

A general outline of the history of the frilled breeds of canary was given in the chapter on the North Dutch Frill where it was explained that, after the mutation had occurred in Holland, frilled canaries gradually spread to other parts of Europe where local variations on the frilled "theme" were developed. The present breed represents one of the creations of Italian fanciers and it is, indeed, a most remarkable one in which the fancy characteristics have been accentuated, in some people's eyes, to an almost unnatural degree.

The precise origin of the Gibber has not been recorded although it would appear to be almost certainly a direct development from the South Dutch Frill with probably no other blood being added. In general appearance there is a very considerable similarity between the two breeds but the Gibber is much smaller in stature, being quite a slim and wispy little bird. Such a diminutive size may have been brought about by the continued use of double yellow matings, which is the normal practice in this breed, or by continuous close inbreeding — or, indeed, most probably by a combination of both of these factors.

At what period these developments took place is not known, although the Gibber is generally regarded as being a relatively new breed and was not recognised by the COM until fairly recently. Very few birds of this variety are kept by fanciers in Britain and they are only occasionally to be seen on the show bench, which is a pity since they are so unusual and quite different from most other breeds of canary.

POINTS OF THE GIBBER ITALICUS

Among the family of frilled canaries, the Gibber is at the opposite end of the spectrum to the Parisian for, whereas the latter is the largest breed and with the most intensely developed frilling, the Gibber is the smallest and with the scantiest of plumage. It is a bird of remarkable appearance and, although perhaps not to everyone's taste, is one of the most distinctive of all canary varieties.

As stated before, the Gibber is a bird that is light and small of frame and with crisp and sparse plumage. In fact, if the feathering is too long and abundant, two of the distinctive characteristics of the breed, a naked breastbone and naked thighs, would no longer be apparent. It is also a breed in which the nervous "twitchiness", that is so characteristic of all frilled varieties, is extremely highly developed; so much so that the bird often seems to totter about on its perches and frequently supports itself by gripping the wires of the cage with one foot.

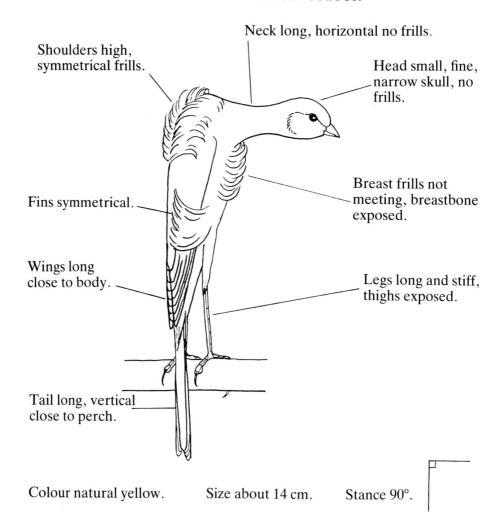

Neck long, horizontal no frills.

Shoulders high, symmetrical frills.

Head small, fine, narrow skull, no frills.

Fins symmetrical.

Breast frills not meeting, breastbone exposed.

Wings long close to body.

Legs long and stiff, thighs exposed.

Tail long, vertical close to perch.

Colour natural yellow.   Size about 14 cm.   Stance 90°.

Position and shape	20	Tail	6
Head	6	Jabot — sternum	10
Neck	15	Flanks	6
Legs	15	Size	6
Wings	6	Total	100
Shoulders and mantle	10		

10.1   The Points of a Gibber Italicus Canary

The head should be small and fine and with a very narrow skull which gives an almost snake-like appearance. This illusion is compounded by the very long neck which the bird can stretch out to the limit when in "position", like the Belgians in its remote ancestry. In fact, like the South Dutch Frill, the Gibber is not only a frilled variety, but a bird of position as well and its posture, in the form of a figure of seven, is highly valued in the Scale of Points. When in position, the body should be completely upright, with a straight back at right angles to the perch, and the head should be thrust well forward at an angle of 90 degrees with the back. The legs are long and stiffly held, with no flexibility at the "elbow", and the long thighs are well exposed and have very little feathering on them.

The feathering, as has already been noted, is short, crisp and sparse and always of the yellow type. Most of the birds that find their way onto the show bench seem to be clears but there is no reason why they should not be variegated or even green so long as they are of the yellow category. The frills of the Gibber, although relatively rudimentary, should still be quite symmetrical and properly formed so that the mantle, craw and fins are clearly in evidence. The breast feathers, however, curling inwards in the usual manner, are so short that they do not meet and thus leave the breastbone exposed — a feature, along with the naked thighs, of this particular breed.

OFFICIAL STANDARDS

The original set-out of the Continental standard that was adopted by the **Old Varieties Canary Association** for use in Britain has since been altered by the COM although the allocation of points for the various features remains the same. Both formats are given below for comparison:

	points
Size: Length 14-15 cm. Well proportioned.	6
Carriage: In the form of a figure 7. Body upright and forming with the line of the head and neck an angle of 90 degrees.	20
Head: Small and fine, narrow skull, small beak, no frills.	6
Neck: Elongated and slender, no frills.	15
Shoulders: High, with symmetrical frills.	10
Breast: Breastbone exposed, frills not meeting in centre.	10
Flanks: Symmetrical on both sides, curving outwards.	6
Legs: Long and stiff, thighs exposed.	15
Wings: Long and straight, held close to body.	6
Tail: Long, vertical, in line with the back, pressed to perch. Rump and vent smooth, no frills.	6
	100

ALTERNATIVE

Head: small, slender, serpent-like.
Breast: frills symmetrical curving inwards naked sternum.
Flanks: frills curving outwards, symmetrical.
Thighs: naked.
Underparts: smooth feathered.
Legs: long and stiff, thighs exposed.
Neck: elongated, slender.
Mantle: curving, symmetrical, to left and right, from centre of back.
Wings: straight and close to body.
Tail: in straight line with back.
Size: 14/15 cm.
Position: forming figure of seven (7), neck extended and square with back.

Although it is not an ancient breed, the Gibber Italicus, along with other continental varieties, is catered for in Britain by the Old Varieties Canary Association.

EXHIBITING THE GIBBER ITALICUS

The type of show cage in which the Gibber is exhibited in Britain is the same as that for all other frilled breeds which, again, is the same as that for the Belgian (which see). Owing to their tiny size, however, it is permissible to have a smaller sized drinker hole in order to prevent the bird from escaping! Perches, too, should be adjusted in size to allow the bird to grip firmly and so give its best posture in front of the judge. Training methods are similar to those already given for "posture" canaries with the additional requirement of having these naturally nervous birds as steady as possible.

Chapter 11

THE GLOSTER FANCY

HISTORY

Unlike the older breeds of canary whose origins are often largely a matter of speculation, the history of the Gloster Fancy has been well documented. It is quite a recent development, as far as the canary fancy is concerned, dating back only to 1925, and is the living proof that the present-day fancier is possessed of imagination and ability no less than his predecessors of earlier generations.

The name of Mrs. Rogerson of Cheltenham in Gloucestershire will forever be associated with this breed for it was she who first exhibited these small sized crested canaries at the Crystal Palace show in 1925. A leading judge of the time, A.W. Smith, recognised them as being something different from the standard Crested Canaries and saw the potential in them for further development into a distinct breed. He was instrumental in drawing up the first standard of excellence and in christening the new breed the Gloster Fancy in deference to Mrs Rogerson's native county. A noted Scottish breeder and judge of Crests, J. McLay, began to co-operate with Mrs Rogerson and, between them, they succeeded in establishing the basic type.

On the authority of A.W. Smith, in his book *The Gloster Fancy Canary,* it is recorded that Mrs. Rogerson's original strain was developed from the crossing of crested Roller canaries with the smallest Borders available, while Mr. McLay's stock consisted of small sized Crests crossed with the early "wee gem" type of Border. It is established, therefore, that the Gloster is the result of a blending of three different breeds but, although it owes its basic genes to the three sources, it has now emerged as a bird quite distinct and different from any of its forebears.

As with most new varieties, the Gloster was a slow starter but its rise in popularity has been steady and emphatic until, today, it can rival any of the major breeds in number in most parts of the country. Like the Border, it is a lively, hardy and prolific breed and is thus well suited to the beginner in canaries on this account although top class exhibition specimens are just as difficult to produce as in any other variety.

POINTS OF THE GLOSTER FANCY

It would be quite wrong to regard the Gloster as merely a miniature edition of the Crested Canary for, apart from the contrast in size, there are many other points of difference. Like all other crested breeds, of course, it exists in both crested and plainhead forms which, in breeding, should be mated together. Nomenclature differs, however, and in the Gloster two fancy names were "invented". Thus, the crested bird is known as a **Corona** and the plainhead as a **Consort** but, apart from the

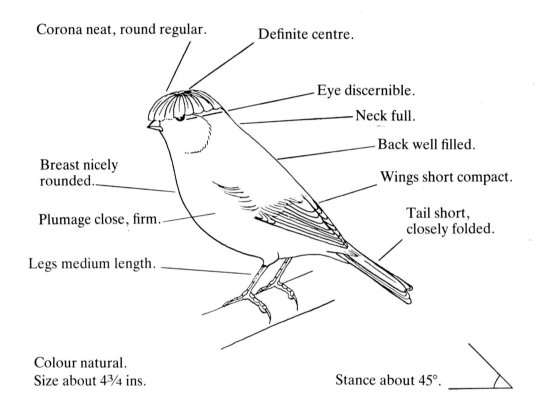

Corona neat, round regular.

Definite centre.

Eye discernible.

Neck full.

Back well filled.

Wings short compact.

Breast nicely rounded.

Plumage close, firm.

Tail short, closely folded.

Legs medium length.

Colour natural.
Size about 4¾ ins.

Stance about 45°.

11.1   The Points of a Gloster Fancy Canary

11.2   Gloster Fancy Canary Show Cage

obvious difference in head properties, the basic body type is the same for either.

The Gloster is one of our smallest breeds, the aims of fanciers always being "a tendency towards the diminutive". No actual statement of size is made in the official standard, however, although about 4¾ inches is often regarded as being the upward limit for a good show bird. In spite of its lack of inches, it is a well-built and "cobby" type of bird, that is to say short and well rounded as opposed to being slim and racy. The body should be quite broad, with a full neck and a back that is well filled. The breast and underparts should also be nicely rounded, in one continuous curve but, although full, not unduly prominent.

Wings and tail should be shortish and carried tightly braced. In the case of the wings, the flights should meet at their tips and not be either crossed or open. The tail should be well carried and not drop below the line of extension of the rump and vent. Legs and feet should be of moderate length and in correct proportion to balance the rest of the body.

Unlike the large Crested canary, the plumage in the smaller bird is of much finer quality. It should be close and firm, giving a good clear-cut outline to the body with no excess of feathering at the thigh or elsewhere. The standard says that they should be "of good natural colour" but Glosters are not notably excellent in this respect as compared with, say, Borders or Fifes. They are to be had in all grades of marking, both in green and cinnamon, and white ground birds are also quite popular. As with the Crested canary, clear bodied birds with dark or grizzled crests are much admired and

GLOSTER CORONA CANARY
Size to be to the diminutive

Standard of Excellence

CORONA:	Neatness, regular unbroken round shape, eye discernible	**15**
	With definite centre	**5**
BODY:	Back well filled and wings laying close thereto; Full neck. Chest nicely rounded without prominence	**20**
TAIL:	Closely folded, well carried	**5**
PLUMAGE:	Close, firm, giving a clear appearance of good quality and natural colour	**15**
CARRIAGE:	Alert, quick, lively movement	**10**
LEGS & FEET:	Medium length, no blemish	**5**
SIZE:	Tendency to the diminutive	**15**
CONDITION:	Health and cleanliness	**10**
		Total 100

11.3 Gloster Fancy Canary
Standard issued by the Gloster Canary Convention

GLOSTER CONSORT CANARY
Size to be to the diminutive

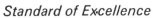

Standard of Excellence

CONSORT:	Head broad, round at every point with good rise over centre of skull	**15**
EYEBROW:	Heavy showing brow	**5**
BODY:	Back well filled and wings laying close thereto; Full neck, chest nicely rounded without prominence	**20**
TAIL:	Closely folded and well carried	**5**
PLUMAGE:	Close, firm, giving a clear cut appearance of good quality and good natural colour	**15**
CARRIAGE:	Alert, quick, lively movement	**10**
LEGS & FEET:	Medium length, no blemish	**5**
SIZE:	Tendency to the diminutive	**15**
CONDITION:	Health and cleanliness	**10**
		Total 100

frequently sccn on the show bench, as well as those with dark crests and even wing marks, but type is the overriding factor and must be the first consideration however attractive the markings may be.

The crest of the corona follows the normal circular pattern which radiates evenly all round from a small, neat centre. The feathers should be of a fair length in order to form a decent and well-filled crest but, since the Gloster is a bird of closer and shorter feather than the Crested canary, it does not reach the stage of drooping down over the beak and eyes as with the larger breed. The frontal feathers, however, should at least reach the end of the beak and the standard states that the eye should be "discernible". There should, of course, be no bald spot of skin showing and no break in the regularity of the radiation of the crest feathers. Likewise, the unfortunate defects of tufts and horns, and any roughness at the back of the crest, are all to be avoided.

In the case of the consort, the head should be bold and well rounded, with a definite rise over the top of the skull, and there should be a decided fullness over the eye but without any tendency towards the overhanging eyebrows as seen in the Crestbred or Lancashire Plainhead canaries.

EXHIBITING THE GLOSTER FANCY CANARY

Beyond the normal show cage training that is needed for all varieties, little need be done in the way of any special preparation. The Gloster is not judged for such things as posture, or position, although 10 pints are allowed in the Standard for carriage, which, in this case means a free and lively movement from perch to perch as required by the judge. Some Glosters, in fact, are inclined to be a bit restless, moving across the perches and down onto the bottom of the cage almost without a pause, so that the judge has little chance to assess them fairly. Clearly, any such birds need "steadying down" to have any chance of success on the show bench. Another annoying habit that is occasionally encountered is that of travelling the perches quite well but always facing the back of the cage instead of looking the judge in the eye.

The crests of the coronas, of course, must always be shown in good condition. The practice of grooming them with a soft toothbrush dipped in warm water can do much to assist although it will never succeed in curing a basically bad crest.

The show cage used for the Gloster is an adaptation of the older Crested canary show cage made more suitable for the smaller breed. It is a cage of the box type in which the wire front is curved backwards, or "bowed", at the top which thus allows the judge more easily to inspect the crest from above. The cage is 12 inches in length, 10 inches in height and 4¾ inches in depth. It is painted in black on the wires and the outside, the inside being in eau-de-nil*. The wire front should be of 23 wires, with a drinker hole centrally placed, and the drinker itself, which is of the common "D"-shaped show cage pattern, should also be in black.

There is a seed trough situated at floor level on the right hand side just below the door and the two perches should be ⅜ inches in diameter. The floor covering while the birds are at a show should be of seed.

*This colour is now discontinued as such but its equivalent in B.S. colours is obtainable.

OFFICIAL STANDARD

The official standard is issued by the Gloster Convention and is as follows:

STANDARD OF EXCELLENCE

	Points
Corona: Neatness, regular unbroken round shape, eye descernible	15
With definite centre	5
Body: Back well filled and wings laying close thereto;	
Full neck. Chest nicely rounded without prominence.	20
Tail: Closely folded, well carried.	5
Plumage: Close, firm, giving a clear appearance of good quality and natural colour.	15
Carriage: Alert, quick, lively movement.	10
Legs & Feet: Medium length, no blemish.	5
Size: Tendency to the diminutive.	15
Condition: Health and cleanliness.	10
	Total 100

STANDARD OF EXCELLENCE

	Points
Consort: Head broad, round at every point with good rise over centre of skull.	15
Eyebrow: Heavy showing brow.	5
Body: Back well filled and wings laying close thereto;	
Full neck, chest nicely rounded without prominence.	20
Tail: Closely folded and well carried.	5
Plumage: Close, firm, giving a clear cut appearance of good quality and good natural colour.	15
Carriage: Alert, quick, lively movement.	10
Legs & Feet: Medium length, no blemish.	5
Size: Tendency to the diminutive.	15
Condition: Health and cleanliness.	10
	Total 100

The Gloster Fancy now has around 24 specialist societies to its name which, together, form the Gloster Convention.

77

12.0   Examples of Early Lancashires, Plainhead and Coppy

Chapter 12

THE LANCASHIRE

EARLY HISTORY

The origin and the early history of the Lancashire canary have never been documented but eminent Victorian authorities on canaries, relying on verbal information handed on by successive generations of fanciers, have stated that it was evolved from stocks of the Old Dutch strain, previously referred to in other connections, that were brought to this country by Flemish weavers during the eighteenth century.

It had evidently become a well established type by the 1820's or 1830's and probably reached the peak of its development as a breed by late Victorian times. At this period, some writers preferred to call it the "Manchester Coppy" because many of its breeders were to be found within the city but, as it was widely bred throughout the cotton towns of Lancashire, it was clearly more appropriate that the county name should have finally prevailed.

Unfortunately, it never achieved any great following, purely for its own sake, beyond the boundaries of its native county. However, from the late 1870's onwards, it began to be appreciated by fanciers in other parts of the country for the evolution or improvement of other breeds, notably the Crest, the Norwich and the Yorkshire. The resulting inroads that were made upon stocks of Lancashires for these purposes, plus the fact that it was not a notably prolific breeder, resulted in the beginning of a decline in its numbers which has continued almost to the present day.

Although there is no actual record of the fact, it is thought probable that the last pure-bred stocks of Lancashire became extinct during the second world war since there were still a few Lancashires around in 1939 but, apparently, none at all were traceable in the late 1940's. There the matter may have ended but, fortunately, the various breeds to which it contributed its genes in the past are still with us and, with the revival of interest in the old breeds of canary, it has been possible by carefully considered breeding programmes, to re-create the Lancashire once again.

This work, utilising chiefly Crests and Yorkshires, and undertaken mainly by members of the Old Varieties Canary Association, has proved to be quite successful and the present-day Lancashire measures up with a fair degree of accuracy to the standards of former times.

As with all crested varieties, the breed as a whole is made up of the two types of individual namely, those with the crests and their partners with plain, uncrested heads. In the case of the Lancashire canary the crested birds are known as "Coppies" — a curious word for which no adequate explanation exists, the Victorian experts on canaries merely stating that the word "coppy" was an old Lancashire term for a crest. It should be noted, incidentally, that to refer to the breed in its entirety as the Lancashire Coppy (as has sometimes been done) is quite wrong since the word "coppy" applies only to the crested bird so that the breed should be correctly known as the Lancashire Canary. The plain-headed birds are, very sensibly, named from that characteristic and are, therefore, Lancashire Plainheads.

POINTS OF THE LANCASHIRE CANARY

The Lancashire is a most imposing bird for, not only is it one of our crested breeds, but it is also one of the largest, being equalled in size only by the Parisian Frill. As with all crested breeds the bodily conformation is identical in both types and so, apart from their headgear, Coppy and Plainhead should look alike and a description of one will serve for the other.

Unlike the Crested canary, which stands very low across its perch, the Lancashire is one of the upright school. It is a bold and imposing looking bird which should never crouch, nor lean at a low angle across the perch, but always have a commanding, guardsman-like attitude, standing well up on strong legs and feet. In fact, unless it is a big, well-built, upstanding specimen it will have little impact upon the show bench.

As befits our largest native breed of canary, size has always been highly regarded and this has been reflected in the scale of points where as many as 25 points out of 100 are allocated for this feature alone so that, clearly, one quarter of the bird is accounted for by sheer size. The minimum length that breeders aim for is 8 inches and, although some birds fall a little short of this ideal, most of our modern Lancashires can measure up to it without too much trouble and some birds may scale as much as 8¼ inches.

The conformation of the body is very much in keeping with the foregoing characteristics of size and posture; that is to say big and bold throughout. The Lancashire should have a full, thick neck, a broad, well rounded back and a deep, full chest. The body should be long and tapering, finishing in a long tail which may be carried in line with the rest of the body, or drop very slightly, but should never have any suggestion of a "lift" as in the Yorshire canary. The wings, too, should be long and closely folded and carried tightly to the body giving what fanciers term a "long-sided" effect. In all respects, these body features, as described, should be of "massive" proportions — a constantly recurring adjective in the writings of the old time canary experts when describing the Lancashire.

Feather quality has never been considered of any great importance — not surprisingly in a breed where great size is one of the major objectives. In former times, in fact, the birds were often decidedly rough in appearance although, in modern Lancashires, the feather quality is generally of a rather better texture than in pre-war examples.

Colour, too, is of very little consequence. In the old breed the buffs were pallid and the yellows usually no better than a pale lemon shade. As in the case of feather quality, however, today's birds are of far better colour than their predecessors — a characteristic which has almost certainly been inherited from the Yorkshire blood that has gone into their making. On the question of colour, a further important point to be noted by exhibitors is that the Lancashire has, by tradition, always been shown as a clear bird only, with no kind of variegation or body marking being allowed. The sole

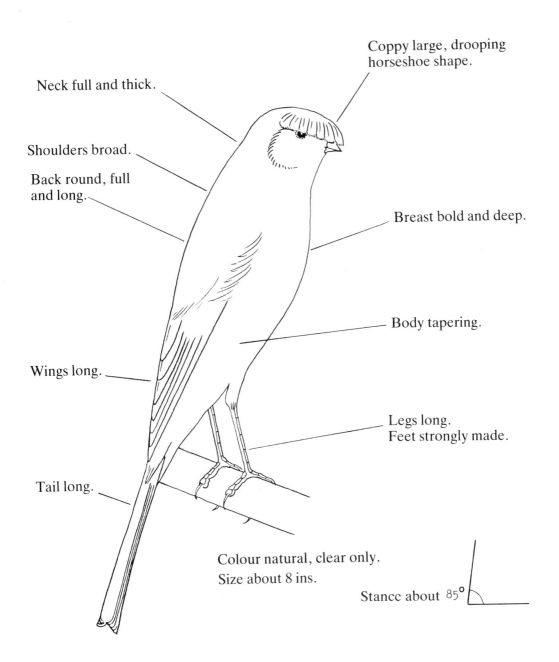

Coppy large, drooping horseshoe shape.

Neck full and thick.

Shoulders broad.

Back round, full and long.

Breast bold and deep.

Body tapering.

Wings long.

Legs long.
Feet strongly made.

Tail long.

Colour natural, clear only.
Size about 8 ins.

Stance about 85°

12.1   The Points of a Lancashire Canary (Coppy)

exception to this is that the crest of the Coppy bird may be grey, or grizzled, without incurring any penalty.

In spite of the importance of all the foregoing description, the feature that is of the greatest significance to Lancashire enthusiasts is the crest which, in this breed, differs somewhat in shape from that of the Crested or Gloster canaries. As in the case of the Crest it can never be too large and, similarly, should consist of an abundance of long, leafy feathers radiating from a small centre on the top of the head. In the Lancashire, however, the crest should be carried well forwards and outwards over the beak and eyes of the bird but, at the back, it should lay well down as closely as possible and merge into the feathers of the neck thus giving the ¾ radial, or "horseshoe", shape to the crest which is the ideal formation for this particular breed.

All of the usual faults to be found in crested canaries are liable to occur in the Lancashire Coppy, too, and thus the breeder and exhibitor are presented with a fascinating challenge in attempting to achieve perfection.

The Lancashire Plainhead, as has been explained, should possess bodily characteristics similar to those of the Coppy. Its head should have overhanging eyebrows giving it the traditional "sulking" appearance which is produced by an abundance of long feathers sweeping back over the crown of the head in a similar manner to those of the Crestbred canary. In fact, the Lancashire Plainhead is to its breed what the Crestbred is to the Crested canary, and similarly, if the head feathers are turned over with a pencil, they should be long enough to reach the end of the beak, or beyond.

EXHIBITING THE LANCASHIRE CANARY

The Lancashire needs a certain amount of training so that it will hold itself up well and show to full advantage when in front of the judge. To achieve this the exhibitor should do all that he can to encourage the bird to stand in as upright a postion as possible; thus, when several birds are run into their show cages for a training session, a sheet of cardboard can be placed between each cage with the height adjusted so that the birds can only just see each other by standing at their full height.

The usual freqent handling of the show cage is also useful when, by gently scratching the bottom of the cage, the bird is alerted to "see what it is all about". As with all methods of training, however, this should not be overdone otherwise eventually the birds will fail to respond.

Care and grooming of the coppy can also be undertaken in a similar way to that recommended for the crest of Crested canaries.

The Lancashire is shown in an open wire show cage with a wooden base, somewhat similar in design to that of the Yorshire; but it is larger, owing to the size of bird for which it is intended, and has a flat top instead of the arched one. The overall height is 14 inches, of which the base accounts for 3 inches, the length is 9 inches and the width 7½ inches. The cage is enamelled black inside and out and has three oval perches, the two lower ones being for access to the drinker at one end and the seed trough at the other. The upper perch is for the bird when in show position.

The drinker is of the usual "D"-shaped, hook on type either of metal or plastic and painted black. No particular kind of floor covering is laid down, except that oat husks are barred, so the exhibitor may use what he pleases in this respect. Experience has

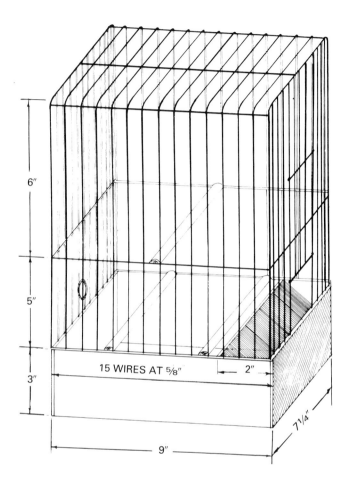

6″

5″

3″

15 WIRES AT ⅝″ 2″

7¼″

9″

12.2 The Lancashire Show Cage

shown, however, that thick white blotting paper is a very satisfactory material for the purpose, as it is both clean and absorbent, and most exhibitors now use it.

In the past, when Lancashires were more plentiful than today, especially at shows within their native county, there were always separate classes provided for Clear Coppies and for Grey or Grizzled Coppies, both in yellow and buff. Today, however, with relatively fewer birds about, all Coppies are required to compete in the same class irrespective of whether their crests are clear, grey or grizzled. Plainheads, nevertheless, must always be shown as clears. There are not, as a rule, any separate classes for yellow and buffs although, at larger shows, there may be a separation into cocks and hens or into flighted and unflighted birds.

OFFICIAL STANDARD

The standard that was adopted for the Lancashire by the **Old Varieties Canary Association** in 1970 is the same as that used by the now defunct Lancashire and Lizard Fanciers' Association which, in its turn, was based upon that of the old Lancashire Canary Association. It is as follows:

"The Lancashire should be a large bird, of good length and stoutness, and when in the show cage should have a bold look. The Coppy should be of a horseshoe shape, commencing behind the eye line and lay close behind the skull, forming a frontal three-quarters of a circle without any break in its shape or formation, and should radiate from its centre with a slight droop. There should be no roughness at the back of the skull. The neck should be long and thick, and the feathers lying soft and close, the shoulders broad, the back long and full, and the chest bold and wide. The wings of the Lancashire should be long, giving to the bird what is called a long-sided appearance. The tail should also be long. When placed in a show cage the bird should stand erect, easy and graceful, being bold in its appearance, and not timid or crouching. It should not be dull or slothful looking, and should move about with ease and elegance. Its legs should be long and in strength match the appearance of the body. When standing upright in the cage the tail should droop slightly, giving the bird the appearance of having a slight curve from the beak to the end of the tail. A Lancashire should neither stand across the perch nor show a hollow back. It should have plenty of feather lying closely to the body and the feather should be fine and soft. The properties of the Plainhead are the same as the Coppy, with the exception of the head. The head should be broad and rather long, the eyebrows clearly defined and overhanging, or what is called lashed. The feather on the head should be soft and plentiful, and not look tucked or whipped up from behind the eye into the neck. The aim in breeding should be to keep and improve the size and length of the bird, at the same time losing nothing of its gracefulness, its beauty of feather and general contour."

SCALE OF POINTS

Head, Coppy.	30
Neck, for fullness and thickness.	10
Back, round, full and long.	10
Length of bird and substance.	25
Upstanding position and type.	15
Condition and cleanliness	10
	Total 100

Chapter 13

THE LIZARD

UNIQUE BREED

Among all of the present-day canary breeds the Lizard is unique in being, not only the oldest of them all, but also the only one that is bred for the pattern and markings of its plumage. These it owes to a mutation in which there is a curious instability of the melanin pigment which disappears from the margin of the feathers as the bird ages. Thus, young Lizards in their nest feathers are not unlike ordinary self-green canaries but, at their first moult when they become unflighted birds, the feathers of the new coat have a narrow edging of a ligher colour which produces the beautiful spangled effect that is a characteristic of this breed. The wing and tail feathers, not being shed at this moult, remain black and in this way the perfect show bird is produced **for one year only.**

Herein lies part of the attraction and challenge of keeping the Lizard for, whereas in most breeds, if an outstanding bird is produced it may continue on a successful show career for many years to come, in the Lizard such as a bird has its one season of glory — or perhaps two at the most — and so fresh show birds have to be bred each year. At the overyear moult white tips appear on the wing and tail feathers and the marginal fringe of lighter colour on the body feathers increases in width. With each successive moult this deterioration in plumage proceeds until, in older birds, the spangling may become hazy and indistinct and the wings and tail quite grizzled. It must be emphasised, however, that such birds are in no way less useful as regards their value as breeding stock and are selected by the fancier on their appearance and show performance when they were unflighted, irrespective of how they might appear in later years.

The origin of this breed and the mutation that gave rise to it have never been recorded but evidently it owes its introduction into Britain to the Huguenot refugees. This assumption is based mainly on some brief information contained in an ancient fanciers' manual called *The Bird Fancier's Guide and Necessary Companion,* dated 1762, which refers to the Lizard, not by its present name, but as, "The fine Spangled Sort . . . which a few years ago was brought hither from France but since much improved in colour and beauty by English breeders." It is, perhaps, worth commenting on that, whatever its origins, the breed must subsequently have died out on the Continent since it was not found there until recent importations were made, although surviving unchanged in form in Britain despite coming very close to extinction during the second world war.

At the present time it is probably more widely kept than at any period in its long history. Although possibly never destined for the widespread popularly of some other breeds, it will always appeal to certain sections of the fancy. This on account of its ancient lineage, purity of blood (it has never been known to have any other breed crossed with it) and for its unique plumage characteristics.

POINTS OF THE LIZARD

The Lizard is, perhaps, best regarded as a dark plumaged self canary, although the presence of genuine light feathers on the crown of the head in the form of a "cap" renders this technically inaccurate. The correct category might be three-parts dark were it not for the fact that birds of this description in other breeds usually have their light areas around the thighs and vent and often have odd white feathers in their wings and tails — all of which are very bad faults in the Lizard. In fact, apart from the cap, the Lizard should have a deep ground colour that is solid throughout its body, wings and tail.

This ground colour has the same basic melanin pigments as any self green canary but more brown may be present since, even in natural colour, the bird is far from appearing a true green but is more of a bronze shade, Actually, the Lizard is colour fed for exhibition purposes and this has the effect of turning the **golds** (the yellows of this breed) into a deep chestnut and the **silvers** (the buffs) into a warm shade of bronze-cum-pewter which is almost velvety in appearance.

Upon this unbroken and evenly-laid background colour appear the most important of the Lizard's features, its markings. The chief of these, carrying 25 points out of 100 on the points scale, are those previously referred to as the **spangling.** Briefly this is formed by a series of jet black, crescent-shaped spots running in orderly parallel rows down the back of the bird starting just behind the cap with quite tiny feathers which increase in size down the neck and reach their largest proportions on the bird's back. These rows of spangles should extend from the back well towards the shoulders where they should not fade away or become indistinct, but form an artistic link with the covert feathers which are also black with a distinct "lacing" of lighter colour around their margins.

Markings of a similar nature to the spangling are also to be found on the bird's breast and these are known as the **rowings.** Owing to the difference in shape of the breast and flank feathers, however, compared with those on the back, these markings are never quite so sharply defined but, nevertheless, should be clear and distinct and again run in perfect lines from throat to tail, extending from both sides of the body well towards the centre of the breast. They are often particularly well developed in silver hens where, in the best specimens, they can be seen almost to perfection.

As in any self canary, the wings and tail of the Lizard should consist of an entire complement of dark feathers which should be as near to jet black as possible. It is a serious fault for any bird to be either "foul-winged" or "foul-tailed", and the presence of any grizzling in the feathers is equally ojectionable and would give the bird little chance on the show bench. The same basic dark pigmentation should extend even to the beak, legs, feet and toenails which should be quite black, although the presence of the odd white toenail is not actually a disqualification but would count against the bird in close competition.

The cap of the Lizard is a most unusual feature of the bird and one that is generally

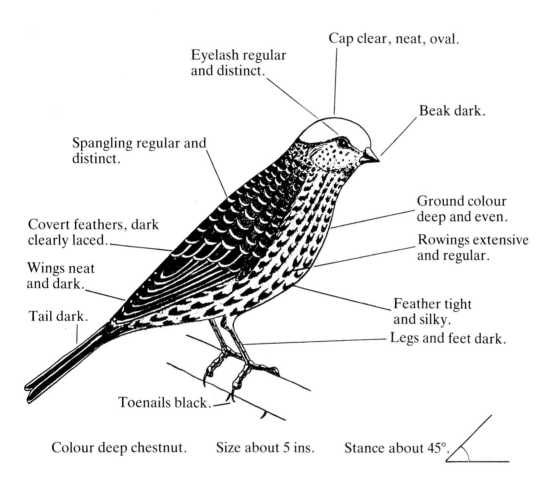

Cap clear, neat, oval.

Eyelash regular
and distinct.

Beak dark.

Spangling regular and
distinct.

Ground colour
deep and even.

Covert feathers, dark
clearly laced.

Rowings extensive
and regular.

Wings neat
and dark.

Tail dark.

Feather tight
and silky.

Legs and feet dark.

Toenails black.

Colour deep chestnut.   Size about 5 ins.   Stance about 45°.

13.1   The Points of a Lizard Canary

13.2   Lizard Canary Showcage

remarked upon even before the spangling. It is a characteristic not found in any other breed and the reason for its presence is not known. A certain amount of research has been done into the genetics involved in the Lizard's spangling but none at all into the inheritance of the cap, which may or may not have appeared as a separate and distinct mutation from the spangling. It is certainly a feature of ancient date for the old fanciers' manual previously referred to makes particular mention of "a Spot on their Heads called by Fanciers a **Cap.**"

In the ideal bird, this feature covers the crown of the head, roughly coinciding with the outline of the skull. It is of an oval, or thumb-nail shape, extending from the base of the upper mandible to the back of the head. It should have a clearly defined outline, without ragged edges, and pass just above the eye from which it is separated by a thin line of feathers called the **eyelash.** This description is of the perfect clear-capped bird and, at one time, no other form was considered as fit for the show bench. However, just as in other breeds, there are marked, variegated and self forms as well as clears, so it is with the Lizard's cap. Thus, within the breed as a whole, there are to be found birds with broken caps and, indeed, birds with no caps at all and so, in the modern system of classification, all are catered for and will be fully defined in the following section.

Lizards are not judged for any particular type but they roughly follow the Border or Fife Fancy in general shape and carriage; in size they fall about midway between these two breeds, being around 4¾ to 5 inches in length. Feather quality is particularly good as, indeed, it should be in a breed where markings need to be displayed to perfection. In any bird of poor quality, the sharpness and clarity of the markings against the ground colour would clearly be quite impossible.

EXHIBITING THE LIZARD

As it is not judged for any special type or posture, the Lizard does not require any extensive training for show. It is most important, however, to have the bird completely steady so that it will not flutter about when the cage is handled. This, naturally, would cause the plumage to become disarranged and consequently destroy the regularity of the markings, at least temporarily until the bird has settled down again. Like most of the smaller breeds, the Lizard is lively and active by nature and so the degree of quietness and steadiness required may need some patience on the part of the fancier.

Great care is also needed in other respects and, in general, Lizards should never be caught in the hand since any clumsiness might cause the loss of a wing or tail feather which, it will be recalled, will then be replaced by one which has a white tip to it. Such an accident is plainly to be avoided, but it is not the end of the road as far as the bird's show career is concerned although, naturally, it would count against it in close competition.

The standard show cage is similar in pattern to that used for Coloured canaries, a plan of which is to be found elsewhere in this book. The colour also is the same, the cage being enamelled black on the outside, with "Summer Blue" for the interior. Perches are not standardised and the exhibitor may choose any pattern he prefers; they should not be too thick in section, however, which would be out of balance with this relatively small canary. The type of floor covering is also optional but Lizard fanciers mostly use several thicknesses of white blotting paper cut to size and this is ideal for keeping the cage both clean and dry.

As explained in the previous section, Lizards are all alike in having no variegation on their bodies and so it is upon the variations found in their caps that classification is based. The recognised categories are as follows:

(a) **Clear Cap** — The ideal is as described in the section on Points of the Lizard but also included is any similar bird provided that its cap has a reasonably regular outline.

(b) **Nearly Clear Cap** — One in which dark feathering may encroach on the cap area, but not exceeding one-tenth of that area in extent.

(c) **Non Cap** — Here the cap is completely lacking and is replaced by normal Lizard-type feathering. The tiny spangles should be just as distinct as those on the neck and back.

(d) **Nearly Non Cap** — Similar to the Non Cap except that some light feathering is present, but not exceeding one-tenth of the normal cap in size.

(e) **Broken Cap** — The whole range lying between (b) and (d) above, namely where dark feathering composes from between one-tenth and nine-tenths of the cap area.

Finally, mention should be made of two cap faults which are considered to be very serious blemishes and render any bird that possesses them unfit for exhibition. The first of these is the **bald-face** in which the cap runs down between the beak and eye onto the cheeks. The second is the **overcapped** bird whose cap runs down into the neck feathers. It is a waste of time to show either type of bird as they would suffer immediate disqualification.

OFFICIAL STANDARD

The Lizard Canary Association has a very detailed description of the ideal bird, prefacing it with the note that, "Golds and Silvers, Capped or Non-Capped, Cocks or Hens, may all attain an equal standard; and that Broken-capped birds which are equal to the ideal in all respects other than the cap will lose only a proportion of the ten points for the cap according to the extent of the blemish."

The description, which is of a clear-capped gold cock is as follows:

"The bird is 4¾ inches in length, neither over-stout nor too slim. It stands quietly and confidently on the perch at an angle of 45 degrees. The ground colour is uniform in depth and is a rich golden bronze entirely free from any suggestion of other shade. The spangling is clear and distinct, each individual spangle being clear of another. It extends from the edge of the cap in perfectly straight lines to the wing coverts, each successive spangle being progressively larger than the one nearer the neck.

The feather quality is of conspicuous silkiness, the feathers being close and tight with no suggestion of coarseness or looseness.

The breast is round and fairly full without giving any impression of stoutness. The rowings are clear and distinct from one another and are lineable. They extend from near the eye down to the base of the tail and across the breast from both sides well towards the centre.

The wing feathers are compact and held closely to the body. Their tips meet in a straight line down the centre of the back. They are so dark, except at the extreme edges, as to appear almost black.

The tail is narrow, straight and neat with feathers of the quality and colour of the wing feathers.

The head is fairly large, round and full on the top. The cap extends from the beak to the base of the skull and is oval in shape with a clearly defined edge. It is clear of the eye being separated therefrom by the eyelash which is a well-defined line of dark feathers extending to the base of the upper mandible. There are no dark feathers between the cap and the upper mandible. The cap is of a deep golden orange and has no blemish of dark or light feather.

The covert feathers are clear, distinct and lineable and so dark as to appear almost black. They are distinctly laced round the edges.

The beak, legs and feet are dark.

The bird is in perfect condition, quite steady and staged correctly."

SCALE OF POINTS

	Points
Spangles. For regularity and distinctness.	25
Feather Quality. For tightness and silkiness.	15
Ground Colour. For depth and evenness.	10
Breast. For extent and regularity or rowings.	10
Wings and Tail. For neatness and darkness.	10
Cap. For neatness and shape.	10
Covert Feathers. For darkness and lacing.	5
Eyelash. For regularity and clarity.	5
Beak, Legs and Feet. For darkness.	5
Steadiness and Staging.	5
	100

"Condition is taken for granted. Any bird which, in the opinion of the judge, is not in perfect health or which shows any physical defect shall not be credited with any points for other virtues.

In classes for Non-capped Lizards points to a maximum of ten are awarded for the perfection of the spangling on the head."

The Lizard Canary Association of Great Britain was founded in 1945 with the primary objective of saving from extinction the few remaining stocks of Lizard canaries. It is still the major specialist society although additional societies of a regional nature have since sprung up as the breed has regained its former status and popularity.

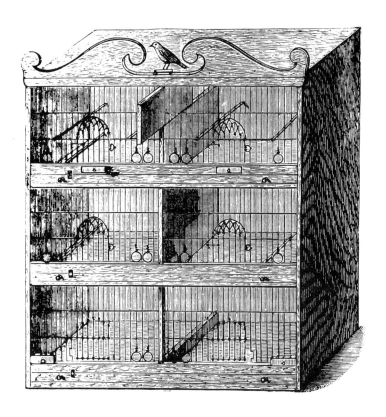

14.0   A Breeding Cage (4 compartments) with Bottom Flight Cage (42in. long and 48in. high). From an old print.

Chapter 14

THE LONDON FANCY

AN EXTINCT BREED

In a book of modern canary standards it may seem inappropriate to include that of a breed that has been extinct for more than sixty years and (in the opinion of the present author) unlikely ever to be revived. However, perhaps nothing should ever be discounted as impossible and so, for the benefit of future generations of fanciers, the facts concerning the London Fancy should be placed on record.

The breed was one of equally ancient date as the Lizard; indeed, it seems more than probable that both breeds stemmed from the same mutation, each one being developed to express a differing degree of the fleeting nature of the melanin pigmentation in the web of the feathers. In the case of the Lizard, as it will be recalled, this disappears from the margins of the feathers at the first moult, leaving it in its elegant, spangled exhibition plumage. With the London Fancy, however, which like the Lizard was an ordinary looking self green bird in the nest feather, the melanin pigment disappeared from the entire web of the feather, leaving the body a clear yellow or buff.

The wings and tail, not being moulted on this occasion, naturally remained their original black and thus we had one of the most beautiful canaries ever to exist, with a golden yellow body contrasting with its black wings and tail. All of this information can be read in the old Victorian books on canaries, although the authorities of those days naturally had no knowledge of genetics and were merely stating matters of fact. Thus it has been left to present day writers to interpret these facts in the light of our modern knowledge.

Many fanciers apparently have completely failed to understand that the London Fancy was, like the Lizard, basically a **self** canary even though the old writers specifically emphasised that, in spite of having an outwardly clear body, the **underflue** remained dark. Thus, to regard the London Fancy as a kind of variegated bird, similar say to an evenly-marked Border Fancy, is plainly in error. Many birds of the breed, in fact, were imperfect specimens and we read that they frequently possessed the remnants of melanin pigmentation in their feathers in the form of faint grey or grizzled markings or as small dark ticks in the centre of the web. Some, indeed, were even more strongly marked and were known to fanciers as "spangle-backs" — a clear indication of their close relationship with the Lizard.

The breed enjoyed its greatest period of prosperity in the early days of fancying and an article was even devoted to it in the *Illustrated London News* in December, 1846. This described the activities of four separate clubs that existed in London at that time and, by way of illustration, there were four engravings consisting of two winning exhibition London Fancies of that year, a Lizard and a Spangle Back. Later in the century, however, the breed was already in a decline, for what reason in unknown, but possibly excessive inbreeding and the relative difficulty of producing a reasonable number of exhibition birds.

By that time, too, and right up to the first world war, fanciers were outcrossing the London Fancy with other breeds in an attempt to salvage their variety but this, if anything, sealed its fate since most of its special characteristics were lost. A few very degenerate specimens of this kind lingered on into the 1920's and 30's but could scarcely be dignified with the name of London Fancy.

From time to time claims that the breed has been revived have been made but these have never stood up to investigation and usually have proved that the fanciers concerned have been somewhat over optimistic, after having produced a few variegated crossbred birds that may have had a few dark feathers in their wings and tails.

POINTS OF THE LONDON FANCY

This, apart from the Lizard, was the only other breed of canary that has been kept for the colour and pattern of its plumage which, as described above, consisted of a clear body with contrasting wings and tail that were dark. It was a "one year only" show bird since, at its overyear moult, the wing and tail feathers were shed and replaced by completely light or grizzled ones — and not just white at the tips as in the Lizard.

In nest feather the bird resembled the young of the Lizard, even to the possession of a cap on the crown of the head (which, again, was specifically mentioned by the old writers) but, with the clearing of the body feathers this would then have presented less of a contrasting feature. Like the Lizard of those days, too, only a clear cap was countenanced, even in those specimens that were less than perfect in body feathering.

The excellent colour of the London Fancy was frequently mentioned by the early writers and this may have been due to the dark underflue which lay beneath giving it a solid background. With the advent of colour feeding, which was adopted by the London Fancy breeders, this colour of course became a golden orange rather than a deep yellow.

As in all selfs, the wings and tail were dark throughout, with no light or grizzled feathers being permissible. Similarly, the horny parts, consisting of the beak, legs, feet and toenails, were all preferred to be as dark as possible.

In size and general type the London Fancy was similar to the Lizard, being about 5 inches in length and standing on the perch at an angle of approximately 45 degrees.

EXHIBITING THE LONDON FANCY

Obviously little need be said on this point, except to state that, when last exhibited, these birds were shown in a cage of similar design and colour to that of the Lizard. Two classes only were then provided, namely one for the **jonques** (the name by which the yellows of this breed were known) and one for **mealies** (the buffs).

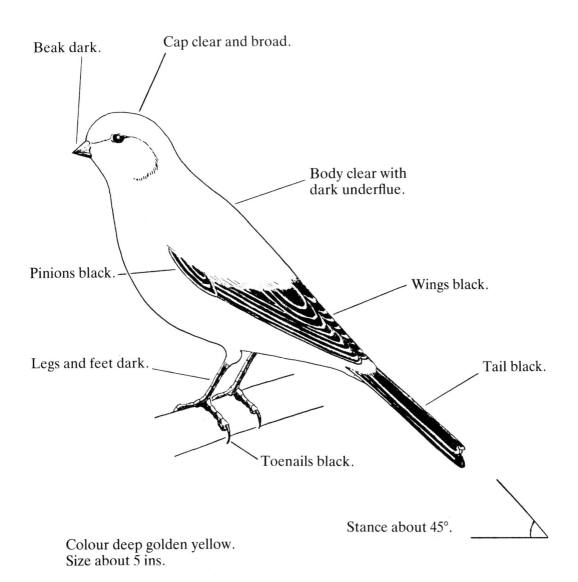

Beak dark.

Cap clear and broad.

Body clear with
dark underflue.

Pinions black.

Wings black.

Legs and feet dark.

Tail black.

Toenails black.

Stance about 45°.

Colour deep golden yellow.
Size about 5 ins.

14.1   The Points of a London Fancy Canary

OFFICIAL STANDARD

The last published standard for the breed was that of the old **London Fancy Club** in 1894. It read as follows:

	Points
Colour: For richness and depth of yellow.	15
Clearness: Clear throughout the body of the bird.	20
Cap: Clear and broad.	5
Wings and Tail: For depth of back, down to the quill, containing not less than 18 flight feathers in each wing and 12 in the tail	25
Pinions and Wing Coverts: For blackness	10
Flue: For blackness.	5
Size: For largeness in conjuction with type.	5
Legs, Nails and Beak: Two birds meeting of otherwise equal merit, preference to be given to dark legs, nails and beak.	5
Condition:	10
	100

If jonque and mealie be equal, preference to be given to jonque.

INFERIOR PROPERTIES

No bird shall be considered a fair show specimen that has a feather or feathers without black in stalk or web in flight or tail feathers.
Entire white feather or feathers in wings or tail.
Deficiency of wing or tail feathers.
Crippled claws, twisted nails, or malformed beak.
Cap broken.
Wings crossed at tips.

Chapter 15

THE MILAN FRILL

The Milan Frill, or Colour Frill as it is alternatively called by the COM, has become established mainly during the past thirty years or so. Originally, fanciers in the Milan area were breeding a pure white frilled canary that was known as the **Milano Bianco** but recently other colour forms have become accepted namely self-blue, which is the equivalent of the self-green in yellow canaries, and clear red orange. No other colour form is at present allowable and the birds must be "unicolore" (i.e. of one colour) with no broken patterns in the way of markings or variegation being permitted.

In type this breed is virtually the same as the Parisian Frill, such minor differences as may exist being on paper rather than in fact. The Milano, therefore, can reasonably be regarded as merely a sub-variety of the Parisian in which the colours have been restricted to the three forms mentioned in the previous paragraph whereas, in the Parisian, all of the usual standard types of colour and marking are to be found.

Few, if any, birds of this breed are to be found in Britain at the present time, most fanciers who are attracted to frilled canaries generally preferring to keep the Parisian.

POINTS OF THE MILAN FRILL

Since this variety is almost identical to the Parisian Frill, the reader is referred to the chapter on the older and more widely kept breed where details of size, type and feather formation are fully dealt with.

EXHIBITING THE MILAN FRILL

The training, preparation for show and type of show cage are the same as for all frilled varieties. Absolute cleanliness is, of course, essential especially in the case of the pure white form where dirty plumage would be particularly apparent.

OFFICIAL STANDARDS

Once again there are minor differences in the standards of the Italian Frilled Canary authorities and those of the COM although, of course, the ideal bird remains the same. Both of the Standards are given below for comparison, beginning with the Italian one.

	Points
Size: Minimum length 19 cm; perfectly proportioned.	10
Carriage: Erect. Head, body and tail in line. Angle from the horizontal about 50 degrees.	10
Plumage: Soft, thick and voluminous. One colour (i.e. white, red orange, blue).	15

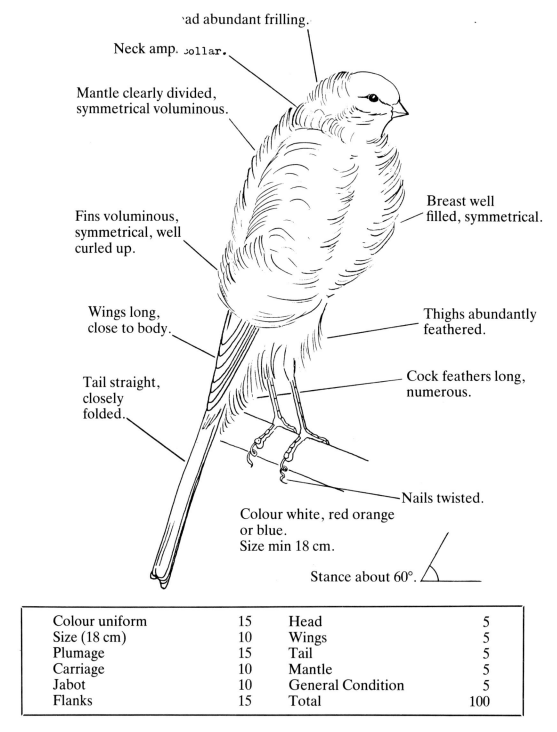

'ad abundant frilling.

Neck amp. ᴐollar.

Mantle clearly divided, symmetrical voluminous.

Fins voluminous, symmetrical, well curled up.

Wings long, close to body.

Tail straight, closely folded.

Breast well filled, symmetrical.

Thighs abundantly feathered.

Cock feathers long, numerous.

Nails twisted.

Colour white, red orange or blue.
Size min 18 cm.

Stance about 60°.

Colour uniform	15	Head	5
Size (18 cm)	10	Wings	5
Plumage	15	Tail	5
Carriage	10	Mantle	5
Jabot	10	General Condition	5
Flanks	15	Total	100

15.1   The Points of a Milan Frilled Canary

Mantle: Clearly divided, symmetrical, voluminous. Well spread and of maximum extension, with "bouquet".   10

Jabot: Well filled, symmetrical, in the form of a closed shell.   10

Flanks: Very voluminous (thick and ample). Well curled up symmetrically and concentrically around the wings.   10

Head and Neck: Head with abundant frilling. Neck with ample collar.   10

Wings: Regular, full complement of feathers, Well carried close to body, neither drooping nor crossed.   5

Legs: Normally extended, thighs abundantly feathered. Legs and feet strong and regular. Nails twisted.   10

Tail: Straight, closely folded, complete. Cock feathers long, numerous and evenly distributed. Rump and vent curled.   5

General Condition: Cleanliness, liveliness, state of health.   5

                                                                                    ———
                                                                                    100
                                                                                    ———

ALTERNATIVE STANDARD (COM)

Neck: well filled.

Mantle: formed by abundant feathers which are divided by a central parting between wings to fall as symmetrically as possible over the shoulders.

Bouquet: continuation of the mantle.

Cock Feathers: falling abundantly on each side of the tail.

Tail: long and robust.

Head: abundant frilling.

Whiskers:

Collar: (neck) — **Bib** (throat).

Jabot: well furnished, forming a shell.

Flanks: (Fins): staring from the femur on each side of the bird to rise concentrically around the wings.

Vent and Thighs: frilled.

Nails: formed like a "corkscrew".

Size: 18 cm.

Carriage: proud and elegant.

Colour: one colour: white, red-orange and blue.

Plumage: soft and voluminous.

Any fanciers who do keep the Milan Frill will find that they are catered for by the **Old Varieties Canary Association.**

16.0 A early type of Crested Norwich
(Quite different from today's *standard* which covers Plainheads only)

Chapter 16

THE NORWICH

AN ANCIENT BREED

To the British public, the Norwich is probably the best known of all breeds of canary, at least by name, and this is no doubt on account of its standing during the Victorian and Edwardian periods of fancying when it was by far the most widely kept variety. Surplus birds from its many breeders readily found their way into the pet shops and street markets of the day, most of them to end up as household pets in thousands of homes, just as the budgerigar is today. Since those times the Norwich has declined somewhat in popularity against the rise of such breeds as the Yorkshire, Border or Gloster, but it still forms one of the major sections at most of our shows.

It is traditionally accepted that the hobby of breeding canaries was introduced into East Anglia by the Flemish refugees from the religious persecutions in the Netherlands during the latter part of the sixteenth century. If so, the Norwich can, indeed, lay claim to an ancient origin although it is unlikely that any development towards a definitive type took place until very much later.

By the middle of the nineteenth century, however, the Norwich had emerged as **the** exhibition breed in England, rivalled only by the Belgian in the estimation of fanciers. The large Victorian works on canaries devoted much space to it and it was well portrayed by the various livestock illustrators of that period. These portraits, together with the descriptive detail, reveal the Norwich of just over a century ago to be quite a different bird from its descendants of the present day, being then much smaller and lighter in build than today's ideals call for.

Since that time two far reaching events altered the whole course of the development of the Norwich canary; namely, the introduction of the practice of colour feeding during the 1870's, and the dramatic change in the basic type that was brought about by outcrossing during the 1880's. The former produced only temporary upsets until it was finally agreed that all Norwich could be colour fed but the change in type eventually led to the establishment of the modern Norwich as we know it today.

It will be recalled that, in the 1870's, the breeders of the Crested Norwich began to make use of the Lancashire Coppy canary to improve their own birds, with quite dramatic results. Soon the Plainhead breeders were following their example by introducing Lancashire blood, either directly through the Lancashire Plainhead, or at second hand from the new Crestbred canaries. Such a craze for sheer size followed that most other features were relegated to a role of secondary importance but, in due time, a reaction against these trends began to set in. This eventually led to the calling of an important conference of fanciers in 1890 where it was estimated that some 400 Norwich breeders were in attendance.

Here, new standards were agreed upon in which type and quality were to be the major considerations and size was to be limited to 6½ inches, and these ideals have remained practically unaltered down to the present time.

POINTS OF THE NORWICH

Although the pursuit of mere size was long ago abandoned, it is still a feature of reasonable importance, for a small, undersized Norwich is something of a contradiction in terms. As far as actual length of body is concerned, from the tip of the beak to the end of the tail, the bird is far from being our largest canary but it is both broad and deep in build so that it possesses a fair amount of bulk and presents the somewhat rotund and stocky appearance of quite a big bird.

The modern type of Norwich should, above all, possess a good head, large and well rounded with great width across the skull in both directions. Ideally, there should be no suggestion of any overhanging eyebrows and the eye itself should be clear and bright. The beak should be short and stout and the cheeks well filled to give the bird a chubby appearance. Any bird with poor head qualities, whatever its other merits, would have little chance of success on the show bench.

The neck should be short and thick connecting the broad, round head almost imperceptibly with the equally broad and well rounded body. This body may be described as exactly the opposite of those breeds that possess a long and finely drawn outline, as it is both short and compact and with great depth through from the back to the breast. The back should be short, broad and almost straight, showing but a very slight rise transversely. The chest is both deep and wide and should be well rounded in one continuous curve from throat to tail.

The wings and tail, following the trend of all the other features, should also be short and compact. As with most breeds of canary the wings must be tightly braced and held close to the body, with the tips of the flight feathers in line, and ending just above the root of the tail. This, too, should be closely folded, or "piped", and must be held in continuation of the line of the body, being neither drooping nor held high in the "robin-tailed" position.

The legs and feet should be strong and well formed and well set back to carry the bird in the normal position of about 45 degrees from the horizontal. Unlike some other breeds, the Norwich is not a bird of position as such but should carry itself well and move quite briskly and not in a slovenly manner.

The old-fashioned virtues for which the original Norwich was famed, namely good feather quality and depth of colour, are still of importance in the breed although now being allotted fewer points than hitherto. The feathering should be short, compact and tight, silky in texture and yet firm, any looseness at the thighs or elsewhere being contrary to the requirements of a good exhibition Norwich. The colour should be as rich and level as possible, being a deep orange in the yellows and an equally deep ground colour, but well mealed, in the buffs. A defect sometimes to be found in this breed is that the yellows may carry a certain amount of mealing, but this should be avoided if at all possible, both in breeding stock and in show birds, or at all events kept to an absolute minimum.

Norwich Canaries are to be had in all of the usual standard canary colours. A small, yet not unimportant, sub-variety is the self cinnamon which at one time had sufficient

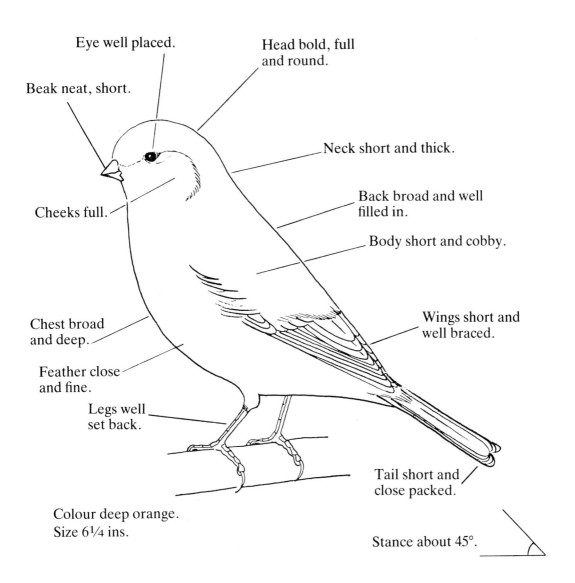

Eye well placed.

Head bold, full
and round.

Beak neat, short.

Neck short and thick.

Cheeks full.

Back broad and well
filled in.

Body short and cobby.

Chest broad
and deep.

Wings short and
well braced.

Feather close
and fine.

Legs well
set back.

Tail short and
close packed.

Colour deep orange.
Size 6¼ ins.

Stance about 45°.

16.1   The Points of a Norwich Canary

of a following to warrant a separate specialist society. At the present time, however, cinnamons are rather neglected which is more than a pity since modern methods of colour feeding can impart a wonderful warm glow to their colouring. Apart from their colour, cinnamons should conform exactly to the normal Norwich standards.

EXHIBITING THE NORWICH

Compared with the majority of breeds, the show training of the Norwich is considerably less demanding, although the primary requirements of confidence and the ability to show itself well before the judge are still as necessary as ever. Lack of steadiness is a fault rarely to be seen in the Norwich which, if anything, has a tendency to be somewhat placid and, perhaps, even lethargic by nature. Because of this, it is advisable to train them to move willingly from perch to perch when required, displaying some life and energy with just the right degree of bounce that a judge likes to see.

The standard show cage, that was first adopted by the Scottish Norwich Plainhead Club, and with which all other Norwich specialist societies have now fallen in line, is of the box-type pattern; that is to say that it is an all wooden construction with the exception of the wire front. It has in addition a sloping false roof which is set at an angle inside the top of the cage. For handling purposes, there is a small thumb-hole 1¼ inches in diameter in the centre of the top of the cage. The full details of this show cage are as follows:

Cage: 12 inches long x 11½ inches high x 4¾ inches broad (all outside sizes) constructed from three-sixteenths inch thick timber. Hole 1¼ inch diameter in centre of roof.

Front: 18 wires ⅝ inch spacing 16 s.w.g. 4th wire from each end at top. Pins between 3rd and 4th wire from each end at bottom. Drinker hole 1 inch square central between 9th and 10th wires.

Door; 3½ inch diameter fitted on right hand side, hinged from rear.

Perches: ½ inch x ⅜ inch, or ½ inch x ½ inch, not tipped or marked, grooved ends to fit flush on bar and 7th wire from each side of front. Material to be of natural wood. It is permissible to round off sharp edges of spars.

Drinker: Standard type zinc or plastic, all black. Zinc natural interior permissible.

Painting: Black exterior. Interior — Meadow Green enamel. No overlays of varnish, etc.

Seed: Plain canary seed only on bottom of showcage prior to completion of judging.

Plate 17

Lizard Canaries – Clear Capped Gold and Clear Capped Silver

Plate 18

Lizard Canaries — Non Capped Silver and Broken Capped Gold

Plate 19

London Fancy Canary — Now Extinct

Plate 20

Milan Frilled Canary – The Original Milano Bianco

Plate 21

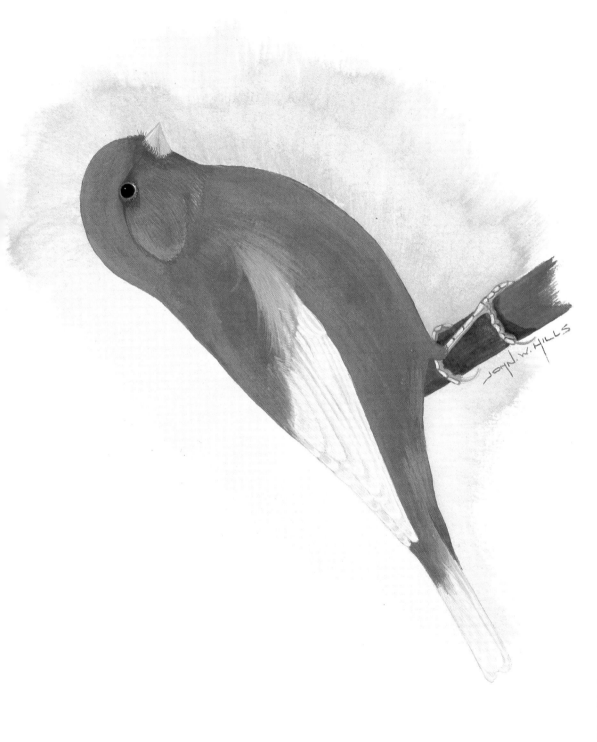

Plate 22

Norwich Canaries — Self Cinnamon and Wing Marked Buff

Plate 23

Padovan Frilled Canary

Plate 24

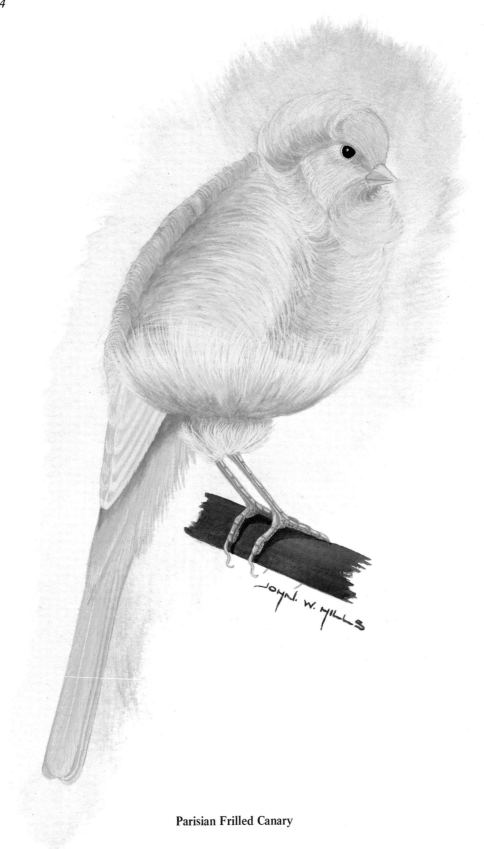

Parisian Frilled Canary

Plate 25

JOHN. W. HILLS

Parisian Frilled Canaries – Variegated and Self Green

Plate 26

Red Canary – Flighted Red Orange

Plate 27

ed Canaries – Clear Apricot and

Wing Marked Red Orange

(both Flighted Birds)

Plate 28

Roller Canary in Full Song

Plate 29

Scotch Fancy Canary

Plate 30

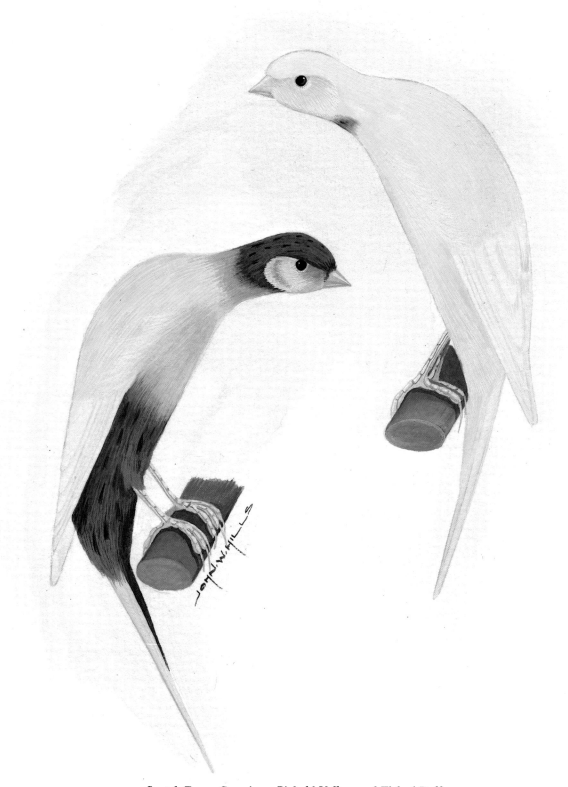

Scotch Fancy Canaries – Piebald Yellow and Ticked Buff

Plate 31

Yorkshire Canary

Plate 32

JOHN W. HILLS

Yorkshire Canaries – Green Variegated Yellow and Cinnamon Variegated Buff

16.2   Norwich Canary Show Cage

OFFICIAL STANDARD

The standard issued by the Norwich Plainhead Club is as follows:

THE STANDARD WITH POINTS

Feature	*Description*	*Points*
Type:	Short and cobby. Back broad and well filled in, showing a slight rise transversely. Chest broad and deep, giving an expansive curved front, and sweeping under therefrom in one full curve to the tail. Ideal length 6 to 6½ ins. Stance or position at about an angle of 45 degrees.	25
Head:	Proportionately bold and assertive in its carriage. A full forehead rising from a short neat beak. To be well rounded over and across the skull. Cheeks full and clean feathered, eye to be well placed and unobscured.	10
Neck:	Short and thick, continuing the run from the back skull on to the shoulders, and from a full throat into the breast.	10
Wings:	Short and well braced, meeting nicely at tips to rest lightly, yet closely on the rump.	10
Tail:	Short, close packed, and well filled in at the root. Rigidly carried, giving an all-of-one-piece appearance with the body.	5
Legs & Feet:	Well set back. Feet perfect.	5
Condition:	In full bloom of perfect health. Bold bouncing in movement.	10
Quality of Feather:	Close and fine in texture, presenting the smooth, silky plumage necessary to give a clean-cut contour.	10
Colour:	Rich, bright and level throughout, with sheen or brilliancy. Yellows a deep orange. Buffs rich in ground colour and well mealed.	10
Staging:	Clean and correctly staged in Standard Club Cage.	5
		100

There are a number of Norwich specialist clubs covering most regions of the British Isles. The breed has a widespread following and nowadays the breeders of East Anglia by no means have the monopoly of the best birds.

Chapter 17

THE PADOVAN FRILL

DEVELOPMENT

This is yet another creation of Italian fanciers which has been developed during the past quarter of a century and named after the city of Padua from which it originated. It was first recognised by the COM in 1974.

Quite simply, it is a frilled canary of more or less Parisian type to which a crest has been added thus giving an attractive combination of fancy features. It is understood to have been "assembled" from the blending of North Dutch and Parisian blood with the crest gene being introduced by means of the Gloster Fancy. One would have thought that the latter would have created problems regarding size and type in the earlier generations but it is quite possible that the perfecting of the Padovan was also aided by an infusion of Lancashire blood. Certainly, in Britain, the Lancashire has been used to improve the size and length of the bird and, at the same time, giving substance to the crest.

According to the Italian authorities, all colours are admissable, preference being given to the colour of the crest contrasting with that of the body so that, ideally, there should be a clear-bodied bird with a dark or grizzled crest such as might be found in the Crested or Gloster Fancy canaries. The COM itself is non-commital on this point, merely stating that the colour should be "uniform", although in describing the crest itself it says that it should preferably be of a dark colour.

For fanciers who wish to keep this variety, it must be remembered that, like all crested breeds, it consists of both crested and plainheaded birds which should be paired up in the usual manner of crest x plainhead to give the genetical expectation of 50% of each type among the progeny.

POINTS OF THE PADOVAN FRILL

The Padovan is a largish bird which stands up well in a bold and fearless manner with the head, body and tail all in line. Like all of the larger breeds of frilled canary, its feathering should be dense and abundant and properly arranged to show each of the basic frills correctly as previously described.

The crest itself follows the usual pattern of crested varieties, being centrally placed on the top of the head and radiating evenly all round from a small centre point. The feathering should be long and leafy, falling well over the beak and eyes, and be devoid of any of the faults often to be found in crests such as splits, horns and so on.

The Padovan crested bird is, of course, quite distinct and different from any other frilled breed of canary on account of its head adornment but the plainhead may easily be confused with either the Parisian or the Milan Frill. The chief points of difference, however, which should distinguish the Padovan plainhead are, (a) that its head and neck should not be frilled in any way, but merely have the distinctive "eyebrows" pos-

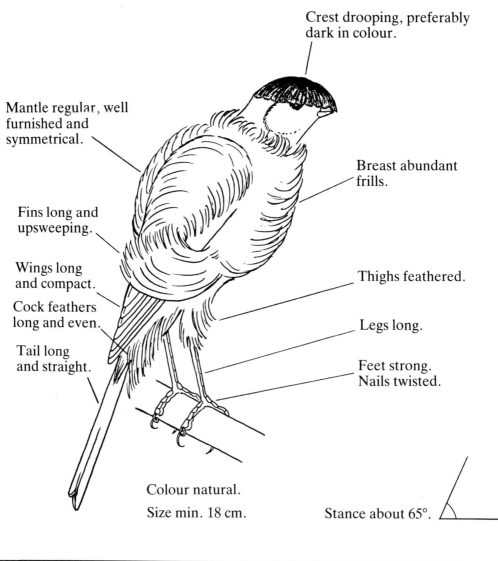

Crest drooping, preferably dark in colour.

Mantle regular, well furnished and symmetrical.

Breast abundant frills.

Fins long and upsweeping.

Wings long and compact.

Thighs feathered.

Cock feathers long and even.

Legs long.

Tail long and straight.

Feet strong.
Nails twisted.

Colour natural.
Size min. 18 cm.

Stance about 65°.

Head and/or crest	15	Fins	10
Colour uniform	15	Wings	5
Plumage	10	Tail	5
Size (17 cm)	10	Carriage	5
Mantle	10	General Condition	5
Jabot	10	Total	100

17.1   The Points of a Padovan Frilled Canary

sessed by the plainheads of other crested breeds, and (b) that its mantle should not end in a "bouquet", as in the case of the Parisian and the Milano, but more closely approach the North Dutch in this particular feature.

Quite often, however, these distinctions are more or less blurred owing to the effects of crossbreeding still being in evidence.

EXHIBITING THE PADOVAN FRILL

Not a very great number of Padovans are kept in Britain at the present time, although one or two specimens are occasionally to be seen at the larger, or more specialised, exhibitions. They should be shown in the same type of show cage as all other frills, as has been previously described, except that a larger drinker hole is permitted in order to prevent any possible damage to the crest when the bird puts its head through to drink.

As well as ensuring that the frills are displayed in an immaculate and undamaged condition, the exhibitor has the added responsibility of presenting the crest as near to perfection as possible. Information concerning the care and grooming of crests can be found in the chapter on the Crested Canary.

OFFICIAL STANDARDS

The Italian standard for this breed is as follows:

	points
Size: Minimum length 18 cm. Perfectly proportioned.	10
Carriage: Erect. Head, body and tail in line. Angle from the horizontal about 65 degrees.	15
Plumage: Silky, voluminous, well arranged. All colours admitted but preference to colour of cap contrasting with that of the body.	10
Mantle: Clearly divided, symmetrical, voluminous. Well spread on each side of the body.	10
Jabot: Voluminous, symmetrical and with feathers from each side converging on the centre.	10
Flanks: Voluminous (thick and ample). Sweeping upwards symmetrically round and beyond the ends of the mantle.	10
Head and Neck: Crest — crest central, symmetrical, with feathers falling over beak and eyes. Plainhead — maximum width of skull, with drooping eyebrows. Neck — visible, smooth and thick, provided around the base with a complete collar.	15
Wings: Regular, full complement of feathers, well carried close to the body, neither drooping nor crossed.	5
Legs: Well extended, thighs feathered and partly showing. Tarsus, feet and nails strong and regular.	5
Tail: Straight, closely folded, complete, proportionate to the body, not forked. Cock feathers clear and symmetrical.	5
General Condition: Cleanliness, liveliness, state of health.	5
	100

ALTERNATIVE STANDARD

The standard of the COM differs in some respects and is given below.

Crest: abundant frills (sic) preferably of a dark colour.

Mantle: regular, well furnished and symmetrical; with a middle parting.

Flanks: starting from the femur on each side of the bird to rise concentrically around the wings.

Tail: long and robust.

Cock Feathers: turning on each side of the tail.

Breast Feathers: abundant frills, forming a voluminous jabot.

Thighs: feathered and "trousered".

Nails: forming a corkscrew.

Colour: uniform.

Plumage: soft and abundant.

Size: minimum 17 cm.

Carriage: proud and elegant.

The Padovan Frill is catered for in Britain by the **Old Varieties Canary Association.**

Chapter 18

THE PARISIAN FRILL

ORIGINS

Not only is the Parisian one of the very old frilled varieties, but it is also the one in which the frilled feathering characteristic has been developed to the ultimate degree, an outstanding specimen seeming almost to be engulfed in its own plumage. The breed dates back at least to the mid-nineteenth century when its progenitors were, most probably, the ancient race of frills that spread from the original centres in the Low Countries into French Flanders. At that period all frilled canaries were known simply as "Dutch" canaries and, as late as 1909, a booklet on the breed published in Paris, was entitled **Le Serin Hollandais Parisien** (i.e. the Parisian Dutch Canary).

As has already been seen, this breed has been the basis for some more recent varieties that have been developed in Italy. Birds of identical type are also to be found in South America and elsewhere. In Britain, the Parisian is easily the most popular of the frilled varieties and quite good displays of them are usually be be found at various major shows in the country.

POINTS OF THE PARISIAN FRILL

In the frilled family of canaries, the Parisian is the counterpart of the Lancashire among the crests; that is to say that it is a big, bold and upstanding bird that immediately demands attention. As has already been mentioned, in this variety the most extreme development of the frilling is to be found so that the two features of great size and boldness, coupled with the intensely developed frills, give to it a most imposing appearance.

In size, adult cock birds should run to about 20 to 21 cm. (i.e. around the 8 inch mark) and should certainly not be less than 19 cm. Unflighted birds may be a little less than this as, in common with most of the larger breeds of canary, they continue to develop after their first year. It must be stressed, however, that mere size, unless it is accompanied by the necessary attributes of well developed frilling, is of no advantage.

The carriage of the bird is described in the old French standard as being "proud and majestic" which means that it should stand boldly upright on long legs and show plenty of nerve and confidence. There are some Parisians, however, perhaps owing to their sheer size and weight, that tend to be somewhat lethargic and inclined to squat on the perch and lean across it at a low angle. This failing was admitted in the old standard description which, nevertheless, added that "at shows the high carriage will always be preferred."

The plumage of the Parisian may range from long, fluffy, billowing feathers, known

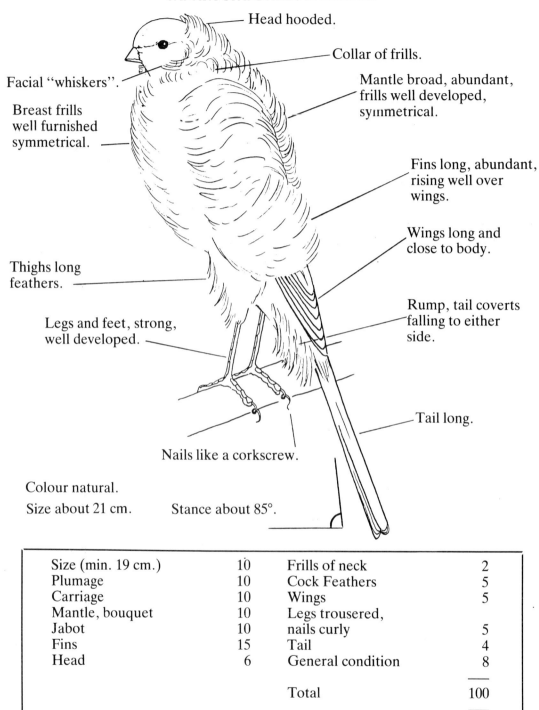

Head hooded.

Collar of frills.

Facial "whiskers".

Mantle broad, abundant, frills well developed, symmetrical.

Breast frills well furnished symmetrical.

Fins long, abundant, rising well over wings.

Wings long and close to body.

Thighs long feathers.

Legs and feet, strong, well developed.

Rump, tail coverts falling to either side.

Nails like a corkscrew.

Tail long.

Colour natural.

Size about 21 cm.   Stance about 85°.

Size (min. 19 cm.)	10	Frills of neck	2
Plumage	10	Cock Feathers	5
Carriage	10	Wings	5
Mantle, bouquet	10	Legs trousered,	
Jabot	10	nails curly	5
Fins	15	Tail	4
Head	6	General condition	8
		Total	100

18.1   The Points of a Parisian Frilled Canary

as "soft" feather, on the one hand and shorter, crisper tighter feathers, known as "hard" feather, on the other. Many birds tend to fall somewhere between the two extremes but the most valued is the long "floating" feather which is so voluminous as to add considerable bulk to the bird's appearance — always provided, of course, that the frills are of the correct formation.

In the old standard the mantle was the highest pointed of all the frills and so, clearly, this is an essential attribute in a show bird. Symmetry is again the key factor and the feathers should fall evenly on either side of a well-defined central parting and wrap themselves well around the shoulders like a cape, giving an appearance of great width at this point. A mean looking mantle is to be avoided, as is one that is too short in length. Ideally the dividing parting should run as far down the back as possible towards the rump and end in a rosette of feathers known as the "bouquet".

The frills on the breast must again be perfectly symmetrical; in other words coming evenly from each side of the body forward over the breastbone and upwards under the throat to form the typical frilly "shirt front". A very bad fault is when the feathers all seem to go to one side only across the chest as though blown to one side by the wind.

The frills on the flanks, or "fins" as they are known, should start from just above the thighs and sweep outwards and upwards concentrically around the wings. The longer and more pronounced the fins are the better and, so important is the appearance of symmetry , that in the old French standard, if a bird possessed one fin only, it was so grave a fault as to entail immediate disqualification.

Unlike the North and South Dutch Frills and the Gibber Italicus, which should have the three basic frills only, the Parisian has been developed to such an extent that it seems to be more or less frilled all over. A careful examination of the bird, however, will reveal that these additional frills are perfectly distinguishable and not just a mere jumble like a feather duster.

Starting with the head, the frills can take on various forms which include (a) feathers falling from the crown on one or both sides to form a kind of skull-cap, or eyebrows not unlike those of the crestbred canary, (b) feathers sweeping up the nape and back of the head to form something like a hood, or helmet, (c) facial feathers with a distinct sweep to them to give a sort of "side-whiskered" effect. Not all birds will possess every one of these features, but the very best specimens do.

The neck, too, has its complement of frilled feathering, this being in the form of a general collar of curled feathers that surround the neck and finish under the beak in a kind of bib that connects with the upsweeping breast feathers.

The lower parts of the body, the rump and the vent (known as the "olive" on the continent), should be long and dense and here is to be found yet another "frill". This takes the form of extra long upper tail coverts which fall on each side of the base of the tail in a similar manner to the saddle feathers of a cockerel and they are, indeed, known to fanciers as "cock feathers".

Coming finally to the legs and feet, there may be found two forms of feathering on the thigh joint. Some birds may possess the normal short and silky type of feather while, in others, the thighs are covered with much longer feathering which even obscures the shanks to some extent (the type known as **culotté** — "trousered"). All other things being equal, the latter would always have preference. Lastly, a remarkable characteristic of this breed is that even the toe-nails grow with a pronounced twist

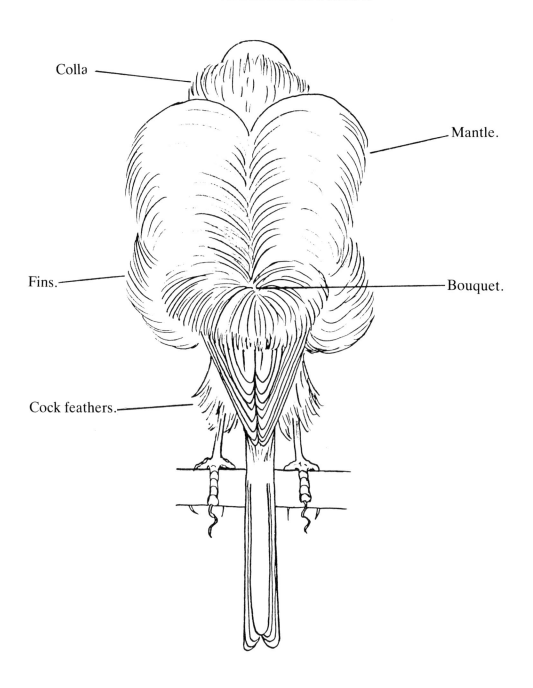

Colla

Mantle.

Fins.

Bouquet.

Cock feathers.

18.2 Parisian Frilled Canary — rear view

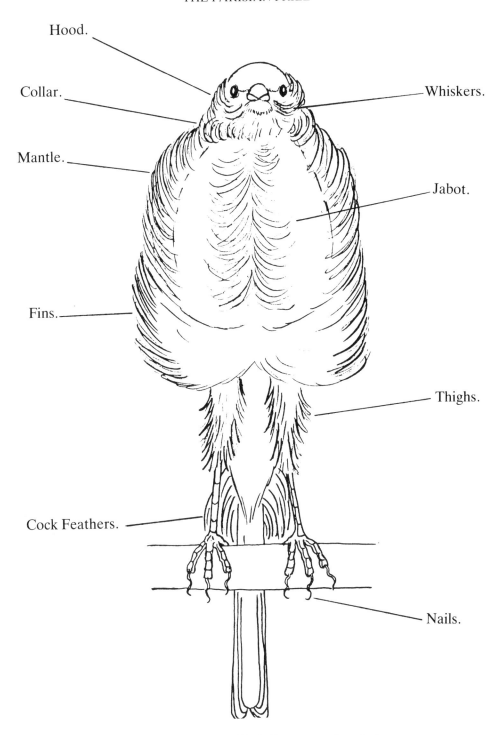

Hood.

Collar.

Mantle.

Fins.

Cock Feathers.

Whiskers.

Jabot.

Thighs.

Nails.

18.3   Parisian Frilled Canary — front view

to them. Not all birds may show this feature but the corkscrew-like toenails are regarded by fanciers as an added mark of quality and purity of breeding.

EXHIBITING THE PARISIAN FRILL

In Britain, the Parisian should be exhibited in the standard frilled canary show cage, common to all frilled breeds, as approved by the OVCA. The type of floor covering to be used in this cage is optional, except that oat husks are debarred, and so this usually means a choice of plain seed, mixed seed or paper (sand or sawdust are two other items that should **never** be used in show cages for any other kind of canary). As an efficient covering that will remain absorbent for several days, two or more thicknesses of plain white blotting paper, or similar, are to be recommended and this, of course, avoids the birds picking up seed from the floor that may well have become fouled.

In common with all other frilled breeds, Parisians tend to be rather highly-strung and so the essential point of having them sufficiently steady in the show cage, without destroying their necessary bounce and nerve, should always be aimed for in training.

Although Parisians are the most widely kept of the frilled varieties in Britain, they are still not numerous and so the classification offered for them at shows is never the extensive one accorded to most of the British breeds. Usually it consists of four classes only, adult cocks, adult hens, unflighted cocks and unflighted hens.

OFFICIAL STANDARDS

The older French standard, originally adopted by the OVCA, is given first followed by the present format of the COM. The points, it will be osberved, are almost the same except that the 15 points have been switched from the mantle to the fins.

	points
Size and Shape: From 19 to 22 cm. Well Built.	10
Feathering: Very even. Fine and long, or crisp and short.	10
Position: Well poised. Massive and symmetrical disposition of the feathers.	10
Mantle: Abundant and well developed, frills reaching almost to the rump, with "bouquet".	15
Breast: Double frills, well furnished and symmetrical.	10
Flanks: Symmetrical with mantle and jabot. Rising well up over the wings and shoulders.	10
Head and Neck: Frills on the head of the helmet or skullcap type. Perfect transition from head to body.	8
Tail Coverts: Falling evenly from the rump to either side.	5
Wings: Long and close to the body.	5
Legs and Feet: Well developed. Nails like a corkscrew.	5
Tail: Long and large. Tips of the quills in line.	4
Condition: Vigorous with poise, General impression massive and symmetrical.	8
	100

ALTERNATIVE STANDARD (COM)

Whiskers:
Jabot: frills long and well furnished adorn each side of the breast to form a shirt front in the form of a closed shell.
Fins: rising concentrically on each side of the bird around the wings.
Olive and Thighs: well furnished with frills.
Head: robust. **Skullcap:** feathers falling on one or both sides of the head. **Helmet:** feathers rising up and rolled in the form of a helmet.
Neck: well furnished.
Collar: (throat, bib, neck).
Mantle: long and well developed frills dividing the back with a central longitudinal parting to fall symmetrically on each side (wings).
Bouquet: continuation of the mantle; an efflorescence near the loins.
Cock Feathers: falling on each side of the tail.
Tail: very robust and large, ending squarely.
Nails: in the form of a corkscrew.
Size: 19/22 cm.
Carriage: erect or crouching.
Plumage: long and fine or short and harsh.

The specialist society for the Parisian Frill in Britain is the **Old Varieties Canary Association.**

Training young birds for showing is an essential requirement

Chapter 19

THE RED CANARY

EARLY ORIGINS

This bird should correctly belong to the section on Coloured canaries but, during the past few decades, it has risen to become an important exhibition variety, often appearing in large numbers where no other coloured canaries are shown. The Red Canary also represents a major advance by breeders of the present century who have succeeded in introducing a factor into the canary's genetical make-up where none existed before. Add to this the fact that there is now a specialist society devoted to the Red Canary only, and it will be appreciated that separate treatment is warranted even though many points in common with other coloured canaries exist.

In the early part of this century, following the publication of Mendel's *Principles of Heredity,* much interest was generated among scientists and breeders alike concerning the possibilities created by Mendel's discoveries. In the field of canaries the name of Dr. Hans Duncker, from Germany was pre-eminent and, as a result of his experimental work, he was able in 1929 to put forward a theory on how a *red* canary might be produced. Briefly this was to be made possible through the medium of another member of the finch family, the brilliant red Hooded Siskin *(Spinus cuculatus)* from Venezuela which had already produced fertile hybrids with the canary, which were of a copper colour, on several occasions.

This, in itself, was a fortuitous occurrence since the majority of mules and hybrids are sterile and Dr. Duncker's theory was that, by back-crossing copper hybrids to canaries again, and repeating this for some generations, the red genes (or "red factor" as it was called at the time) could be handed on until eventually a true red canary emerged. Unfortunately, things did not prove to be quite that simple for, unlike many of the mutant characteristics in the canary which are of a simple dominant or recessive nature and can easily be transferred, the red genes proved to have a more complicated mode of inheritance. Years of patient work were needed by breeders on the Continent, in Britain and in the Americas before true breeding canaries of even an orange colour were to be established and, even today, a genuine red canary has not been bred, although some of the very best examples are certainly of a deep reddish orange hue.

It will, of course, be appreciated that the present breed of red canaries must still be carrying some hooded siskin genes in their hereditary make-up and so, technically, they are not pure *Serinus canaria.* However, since they are hardy and prolific birds and will, in fact, interbreed freely (if desired) with any existing variety of canary, to the fancy in general they are a perfectly acceptable addition to the modern range of breeds.

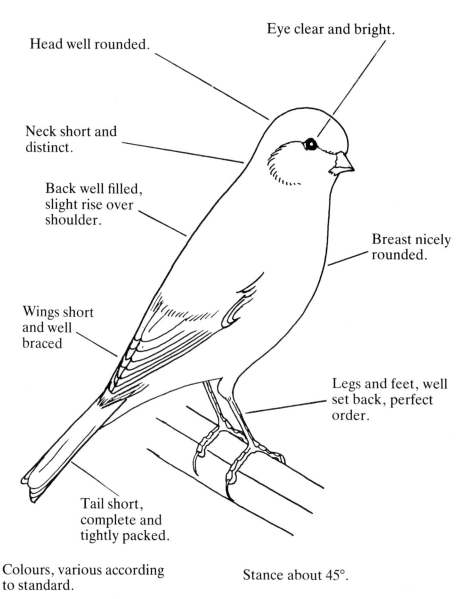

Eye clear and bright.

Head well rounded.

Neck short and distinct.

Back well filled, slight rise over shoulder.

Breast nicely rounded.

Wings short and well braced

Legs and feet, well set back, perfect order.

Tail short, complete and tightly packed.

Colours, various according to standard.

Stance about 45°.

Size about 5 ins.

19.1   The Points of a Red Canary (and all other Coloured Canaries)

POINTS OF THE RED CANARY

It will readily be understood that, in the early years of the Red Canary's development, it was solely the pursuit of red pigmentation that was the breeder's objective and any consideration of type was never allowed to intrude. Standards allotted 90 points to depth and intensity of colour, 10 for condition and staging, and none at all for type. As a result of this, the Red Factor Canary (the name by which it was long known) tended to develop into a rather nondescript type of bird which owed much of its shape to the Roller canaries that formed a large part of its early ancestry.

Nowadays, since the acceptance of the Red Canary in its own right as a show bird, 30 points have been allowed for type and, as a result, the breed has much improved in general appearance. The type that was adopted very much follows that of the Border and Fife Fancy and need not again be repeated here as it is fully set out in the Official Standard section that follows. In size the bird is about the equal of the Lizard, that is to say about 5 inches in length, or midway between the two type breeds mentioned above.

Colour, of course, is still of major importance and should be a bright, fiery, reddish orange, as near to a genuine red as possible. It should be evenly distributed throughout the plumage and should never be dull and brownish, as is sometimes seen. The "yellow" birds of this breed are known either as **intensive** or **non-frosted,** or often merely as **red orange** and they should show no mealing on their plumage whatsoever. However, it is a failing that occurs in this breed that many of them do possess this fault, but at least it should be kept to a minimum and when breeding pairs are being selected it should be on the lines of using only birds that are truly representative of their particular feather types.

The "buff" birds are called **frosted, non-intensive** or **apricot** and, in these, the frosting should appear as in other buff canaries, neither too heavy nor too light and should be nicely distributed over the plumage.

Red canaries are widely exhibited in the clear form, although variegated and self-green (bronze) birds are allowable and are often catered for in the classification at the larger shows. Two other mutant forms possessing basically red pigmentation are also included, namely the dimorphic and the lipochrome pastel (rose), but no other mutations with a red ground colour are at present catered for by the Red Canary Association although fanciers who keep these varieties will find that they are part of the wide range fostered by the Canary Colour Breeders Association.

EXHIBITING THE RED CANARY

The Red Canary needs no specialised training for exhibition but, like most other small breeds, it can be rather restless in its show cage unless steadied down. Efforts should be made, therefore, to accustom the bird to having its cage handled so that it will not flutter about but remain quiet and calm while being examined by the judge. In addition, because colour is all important, absolute cleanliness is an essential for any exhibit since any dirtiness on the feathers shows up to an alarming degree.

An unusual feature of the Red Canary is that the true beauty of the red pigmentation can only be seen at all accurately in a natural light. Unfortunately, many show

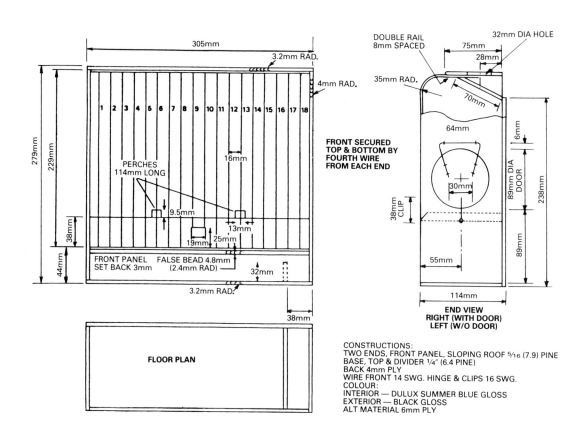

305mm

3.2mm RAD.

4mm RAD.

DOUBLE RAIL
8mm SPACED

32mm DIA HOLE

75mm

28mm

35mm RAD.

70mm

1 2 3 4 5 6 7 8 9 10 11 12 13 14 15 16 17 18

FRONT SECURED
TOP & BOTTOM BY
FOURTH WIRE
FROM EACH END

64mm

279mm

229mm

PERCHES
114mm LONG

16mm

9.5mm

89mm DIA
DOOR

238mm

30mm

6mm

38mm
CLIP

13mm

25mm

19mm

89mm

38mm

44mm

FRONT PANEL   FALSE BEAD 4.8mm
SET BACK 3mm   (2.4mm RAD)

32mm

55mm

3.2mm RAD.

114mm

38mm

**END VIEW
RIGHT (WITH DOOR)
LEFT (W/O DOOR)**

FLOOR PLAN

CONSTRUCTIONS:
TWO ENDS, FRONT PANEL, SLOPING ROOF 5/16 (7.9) PINE
BASE, TOP & DIVIDER ¼" (6.4 PINE)
BACK 4mm PLY
WIRE FRONT 14 SWG. HINGE & CLIPS 16 SWG.
COLOUR:
INTERIOR — DULUX SUMMER BLUE GLOSS
EXTERIOR — BLACK GLOSS
ALT MATERIAL 6mm PLY

19.2   Red Canary Show Cage

halls nowadays have fluorescent tube lighting of the "daylight" type which destroys the glowing red colour to a considerable degree so that visitors to the show seldom are able to see the Red Canaries at their best. It is reassuring to know, however, that at judging time any competent judge will insist that he has his judging bench positioned in a good natural light so that he can make his awards with some precision.

A new design of show cage especially for the Red Canary has recently been adopted, the specifications for which are reproduced in Fig. 19.2. Care should be taken in seeing that these are strictly adhered to otherwise the bird could be at a disadvantage in close competition, especially when the awarding of "specials" are involved.

OFFICIAL STANDARD

The official standard for the Red Canary follows very closely that of the Coloured Canaries but, as there are several variations particularly applicable to the Red, it is here given in full.

STANDARD OF EXCELLENCE

1. **Points**

Clear, ticked &	Colour	50
Variegated.	Degree of Frosting	10
	Type	30
	Condition and Feather Quality	10
		100

Bronze.	Lipochrome Colour	25
	Melanistic Colour	25
	Degree of Frosting	10
	Type	30
	Condition and Feather Quality	10
		100

A total of up to 20 points can be deducted by the Judge from an exhibit staged in a dirty or non standard cage.

2. **Specific Standards**
   1. The pictorial model will apply.
   2. The ideal length of a Red Canary is 5 inches.
   3. Lipochrome Colour.
      a. Red Colour to be bright fiery red evenly distributed throughout the plumage.
      b. Rose to be bright deep rich pink evenly distributed throughout the plumage.

3. **General Faults Covering Lipochrome Colours**
   1. Uneven depth and distribution of colour.
   2. Dullness in colour.
   3. Insufficient depth of colour.

4. **Melanistic Colouring**
   Melanins to be distinct over the head, back and flanks, progressing round into the chest area. Optical blue (reduction of brown) factor to be present.
   Faults:
   - a. Pencilling too coarse or faint and/or missing from flanks.
   - b. Light coloured feet, legs and beak.
   - c. No foul birds or areas of variegation to be allowed in self birds. A bird with such faults to be immediately disqualified.

5. **Degree of Frosting**
   - a. **Intensive** All birds, ideally, should show no frosting whatever but, when this is present, it must be kept to an absolute minimum.
     Faults: Too much frosting, particularly on the back and flanks.
   - b. **Apricot** clear distinct frosting being neither too coarse nor too fine should be present and evenly distributed over the whole plumage.
     Faults: Irregular distribution of frosting often seen as either a frost free chest or a heavily frosted neck and back.
   - c. **Dimorphic** Must show the requirements of dimorphism, i.e. only four colour points; face, shoulders, rump and chest. To be more specific, these areas are itemised further.
     Face: Hens to show "eyebrows" only. Colour not to run from eye to eye nor down the cheeks.
       Cocks to show a blaze typical of a Goldfinch, i.e. an area of colouration extending centrally from the beak and should be as restricted as possible.
     Shoulders: Small distinct area on the shoulders only. Colour not to extend to the wing flights.
     Rump: Small distinct area on top of the rump, not to extend to back or under body.
     Chest: Slight area centrally on chest, not to flow up or down to head and under body.
     Remainder of body plumage, wings and tail to show bright, clean white.

   The colour points of the cocks will be enlarged in comparison to the hens.
   Faults: (Hens particularly)
   - a. Colouring above beak, on forehead, between beak and breast, running into wing flights.
   - b. Rough feathering.

6. **Feather Quality and Condition**

Plumage to be close and firm in texture, presenting a smooth silky appearance giving a clear cut contour to the body. The bird to be in full bloom of perfect health, clean, jaunty, bouncing in a steady manner.

7. **Type**
   a. **Body Outline.** Short and full to conform with agreed outline. Back well filled in showing a slight rise transversely. Chest broad and full, giving a nicely rounded front at an angle of 45 degrees approximately to the perch.
   b. **Head.** A full forehead rising from a short, neat beak, to be well rounded over and across the skull. Eyes distinct, clear and bright.
   c. **Neck.** Short and distinct, flowing neatly from back of skull onto shoulders and from full throat into breast.
   d. **Wings.** Short and well braced meeting nicely at tips to rest lightly, yet closely, on rump. (Tips of wings to end on rump). Flights to rest together, neatly tapering off gradually along wings.
   e. **Tail.** Complete, short and tightly packed, well filled in at the root. To be carried rigidly, giving an all in line appearance to the body.
   f. **Legs and Feet.** Legs well set back, free from scale, feet perfect, all nails showing.

8. **Individual Standards**

Variegation is permitted with the exceptions of the Dimorphic and the Bronze. Variegation is defined as follows:

Clear: A bird showing no melanistic pigmentation in its plumage whatever.

Ticked: A bird with one dark mark in its plumage coverable by a one penny piece.

Variegated: A bird having either more than one ticked mark or melanin pigment in excess of that coverable by a one penny piece, up to a self bird with one foul feather.

N.B. 1. Dark colouration on the horny areas must be discounted.
   2. In all classes where a clear bird is considered equal in all areas to a ticked or variegated bird, the clear will take preference.

In Britain, the Red Canary is specifically catered for by the Red Canary Association but is also included in the classfication of the Canary Colour Breeders Association with its many regional societies.

20.0   The "Hartz" Canary or German Whistler

Chapter 20

THE ROLLER

A SONG BIRD

The Roller canary fancy forms a quite separate and distinct section in the world of canaries and Roller shows, or contests as they are more correctly known, are never held in conjuction with other bird shows. This is because (a) the Roller fancier, in general, has little interest in the type or colour breeds in any case and, more importantly, (b) so that the Roller's song, so carefully cultivated and trained, will not be impaired by picking up undesirable notes from the other birds. For the sake of completeness, a chapter on the Roller has been included in this book of Canary Standards, even though their standards are of an entirely different nature, in the hope that the "type" men may come to have a little understanding of the special problems confronting the Roller fancier.

Insofar as the wild canary was originally prized for the quality of its song, the ideals of the Roller fancy may be said to have had the very earliest of beginnings. The song of the present-day contest Roller, however, has about as much in common with the original wild-type of song as the shape of, say, the Scotch Fancy has to that of the wild birds of those islands. This song has been arrived at by an equally long period of development, involving careful selection, breeding and training, and it is principally to the canary fanciers of Germany that we owe the existence of the Roller canary as a separate breed today.

Quite early in the bird's domestication it was observed that some were superior songsters to the general run of the species, also that many had the ability to assimilate the notes of other birds into their own song passages. Young birds, therefore, were often placed under the "tutorship" of such acknowledged songsters as the nightingale, woodlark, and so on, in the hope of improving their song. Later on, musical instruments such as the flute were employed to extend its range and quality and, eventually, perhaps not surprisingly, some ingenious fancier had invented a device known as a "bird organ" which was capable of producing a variety of trilling, rolling and bubbling notes as required!

Although all of this early development took place during the eighteenth century, it is interesting to note that the soundness of its principles have quite recently been fully endorsed by experimental work on bird song. This has shown that young cock birds of any species, brought up in complete isolation, will still sing, without any tuition, the rudimentary basics of the song of their own kind; yet they do need the assistance of an adult in order to develop its full expression. In other words, bird song is partly inherited and partly learned.

In due course, by means of careful training and the selection of the most accomplished birds for breeding stock, strains of these "artificial" songsters were gradu-

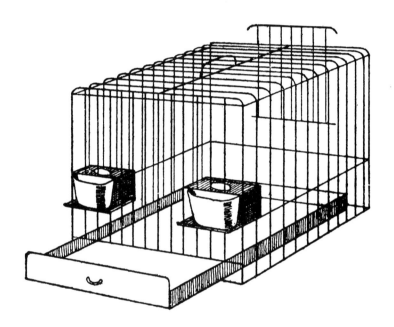

20.1   Roller Canary Singing or Training Cage

ally developed, especially in the region of the Hartz Mountains, which eventually became the centre of a considerable export trade from Germany which, at its height, was estimated to consist of at least half a million birds being sent out annually to other parts of Europe and the Americas.

Britain has always been the the stronghold of the type breeds of canary, but the Roller is still the most widely kept variety on the Continent and in the Americas. Here, it has a smaller, but no less enthusiastic following which is confined, naturally, to those who have a sufficiently well developed musical ear to enable them to appreciate the small differences in pitch and tonal quality of bird song that is not normally possessed by the majority of fanciers.

POINTS OF THE ROLLER

It will, of course, be appreciated that the outward appearance of the Roller counts for nothing and it is solely upon its song that it is valued. As a result of this, the general type of the bird differs little from that of the wild canary and, for many years, the majority of them were still of the self-green, foul or variegated range of markings. More recently, however, possibly in an attempt to render their birds more attractive in appearance, other colours such as clear yellow, orange or white have been introduced, although the real old-time fancier will often insist that greens are still the superior songsters!

The song, as has already been said, differs entirely from that of any other canary and basically consists of a melodious warbling, or trilling, rising and falling in pitch and tempo, and delivered in a continuously rolling manner that has given the breed its name. Experts have registered fourteen different song passages (one of them now acknowledged to be extinct) each of which constitutes a distinctly recognisable melodic entity, and each bearing a name, which in some cases is the original German one where this is not easily translatable.

The Roller's song comes from deep in the throat and is delivered with an almost closed beak so that the sound emerging is always restrained and well controlled. It may vary in volume from little more than a whisper to much louder passages, but the bird never "lets go" with the noisy, harsh, "chop-chop-chop" type of song typical of the majorty of canaries. The song passages are divided into **rolls** and **tours,** the difference between them being in the tempo of their delivery. The rolls, for example, have so fast a beat as to be almost inseparable to the human ear and may be likened, in a general way, to whistling a note while, at the same time, vibrating the tongue rapidly behind the upper teeth, thus: *whrrrrrr.* The tours are passages delivered at a slower tempo in which the beats are easily registered and recognised by the human ear. The rolling passages consist of Hollow Roll, Bass Roll, Bell Roll, Water Roll and Glucke Roll. The tours are Glucke, Water Glucke, Hollow Bell, Schockel, Flutes, Bell, Deep Bubbling Water Tour and the now extinct Koller.

The compass of the Roller's song is said to have been measured at about three octaves, although this does not mean that all birds possess that kind of range. Some song passages may be rendered in more than one register as, for example, Hollow Roll, Bass Roll, Glucke, Water Glucke, Glucke Roll and Schockel, which the bird may sing in the bottom or middle registers. Bell Roll and Bell Tour, however, can only be sung in the top register and Flutes, alone, may be rendered in all three registers.

The **tone** of the bird's song is determined by the quality of the vowel sounds being uttered, as in the human voice (try, for example, singing the same note to "ooh", "aah", "aye" and "eee"!). In general terms the richer vowels are the more highly valued, the order of merit being U. O. A. I. E.

So much for a brief analysis of the basics of the Roller's song (very difficult to explain in mere words) but the final effect must be one of perfect balance and a pleasing song with musical cadences that are satisfying to the judges ear. Not all birds are capable of singing *every* song passage by any means, but quality, rather than mere variety, is usually the final arbiter in these matters.

EXHIBITING THE ROLLER

As explained previously, shows involving Roller canaries are in the form of song contests in which the birds are awarded points by the judge according to the excellence, or otherwise, of their rendering of the various song passages. This in itself is a most exacting task for, whereas, a type judge can usually quite quickly dismiss the "also rans" from his classes before concentrating upon the major placings, the Roller judge must listen to every bird. For this reason, no judge is permitted to adjudicate upon more than sixty-five birds in one day; moreover, Roller judges are required to have taken and passed a judges examination to ensure their competence.

The Roller fancier has a long and quite arduous period of training for his birds to undergo before they are finally fit for contest. It begins by segregating the young cocks as soon as they commence to warble, preferably putting them into a separate room along with an experienced adult cock who is singing well at the time. This bird is known as a "schoolmaster", or "tutor", and from him the youngsters are expected to perfect their own song. The birds are kept in a semi-darkened state so that they can concentrate upon their song and not be distracted by other things. As soon as possible they are caged singly and a "listening watch" is kept so that any youngster who happens to develop faulty notes can be removed at once in case the offending rendition is copied by the others.

Later training involves placing the young songsters in their contest cages, which have shutters on the front that can be closed so that the bird is in darkness. The idea is, that when the shutters are opened up, the bird should start to sing within a very few minutes. At contests, the judge will allow up to 30 minutes, after which, if the bird has failed to sing, "N.S." (No song) will be recorded on his judging sheet. Standard contest cages only may be used and must be presented in a sound and clean condition.

The outside dimensions of these cages are 11⅛ inches high, 10 inches wide and 5½ inches from back to front. Two perches ½ x ⅜ inches, with chamfered edges, are fixed horizontally from back to front and positioned on the bar between the third and fourth wires from each vessel, shutters held closed by the official fastener. The cage to be painted black on the outside and Meadow Green or Sea Green (B.S. 381/217) inside. Natural coloured sponges must be used in the water vessel on the right hand side. Basic seed in the left hand vessel is the only food permitted. Cage labels must be affixed as follows; one on the outside of the cage horizontally and central on the right hand shutter, the other on the inside on the bottom front rail, again horizontally and centrally placed.

Classes are provided in Roller contests for current year birds as follows: Class "A" for exhibitors of Champion status, and Class "B" for exhibitors of Amateur status. In addition, for any age birds, a Class "D" is provided and caters for exhibitors of either status. All contest Rollers are required to be **close rung** with the rings issued by the controlling authority, or the rings of some other reputable Roller canary authority that is considered acceptable, and the birds must be the bona fide property of, and bred and trained by, the exhibitor. From all of the foreging data it can be seen that the breeding, training and exhibiting of Roller canaries is a somewhat exacting (though nevertheless fascinating) procedure.

OFFICIAL STANDARD

In Britain it will be appreciated that, in a sense, all Roller clubs are specialist societies since they are devoted to the one breed only. All of them are affiliated either to the **British Roller Canary Association,** if in the northern half of the country, or to the **National Roller Canary Society** if in the midlands or south. Both associations have the same judging standards and there is but one body of judges, known as the Association of Roller Canary Judges, who are empowered to officiate at any of the contests that are held.

A copy of the type of judging sheet used, which also indicates the maximum number of points allowed for each roll and tour is printed on the following page.

BRITISH ROLLER CANARY ASSOCIATION

PRIZE	CLASS	Number in Catalogue	Hollow Roll 11	Bass 11	Water Glucke 10	Glucke Roll 10	Glucke Bell 10	Hollow Bell 8	Schoc-kle 8	Flutes 8	Water Roll 6	D.B. W.T. 5	Roll Bell 3	Bell Tour 2	General Effect 10	Total Good Points	Faulty Glucke 6	Faulty Flutes 6	Hard Aufzug 3	Bad Nazal Tour 6	Faulty Bells 6	Ugly Inter-jections 6	Total-Faults	GRAND TOTAL	JUDGE

Mr. _____

Date _____

Hon. Sec. _____

20.2   Roller Canary Song Contest Scoring Sheet

Chapter 21

THE SCOTCH FANCY

HISTORY

The origin of so unusually shaped a bird as the Scotch Fancy Canary might well give cause for speculation since it is quite different in appearance from all other British breeds. A leading authority on canaries in Victorian times, W.A. Blakston, was in no doubt about the matter however, firmly stating that it had been developed from imported Belgian stock (i.e. the **postuurvogel)** during the early part of the nineteenth century.

By the 1830's evidently a quite distinct type of bird was being bred by fanciers in the Glasgow area where it was known by the local name of "Glasgow Don". Such was the following for the breed that, apparently, no other variety was deemed worthy of attention in Scotland in those days and writers like Blakston mention exhibitions of these birds in the late 1870's where classes of 50 or 60, and overall totals of several hundreds, were a common occurrence.

The change that took place in the development of many breeds during the expansion of the canary fancy in the latter part of the nineteenth century was also to have its effect upon the Scotch Fancy whose breeders, like others, began to look for improvements in their birds from outside the breed. For this, they turned once again to the Belgian canary which, by now, had become a very highly developed fancy variety and was at the peak of its popularity. The changes that were effected by this outcrossing were eventually so great that the "new" Scotch Fancy became almost a different breed and caused one of the great Victorian writers, R.M. Wallace, to add a fresh chapter to the third edition of his "Canary Book" in 1893 which he entitled "The Modern Scotch Fancy".

In fact, the extensive use that was made of Belgian blood resulted in a Scotch Fancy that so closely resembled the Belgian that, apparently, it was sometimes difficult to tell the two breeds apart. One well-known writer, just before the first world war, went so far as to say that it frequently happened for a bird to be shown with equal success as either variety!

Clearly, this was a most unsatisfactory state of affairs and it is, indeed, from about this period that the beginning of a decline in the fortunes of the Scotch Fancy can be traced — a process that has continued right down to the present time.

In the hands of a very few fanciers, the remnants of the breed survived during the between-wars period but, following the second world war and with an inactive specialist society, it was left to the newly formed Old Varieties Canary Association to mount a "rescue operation". After consultation with all fanciers who were known to be still interested in the welfare of the breed, it was decided to return to the older standard once again in order to try to recapture the popularity of this truly fancy variety of canary.

So far, a very encourgaging degree of success has been achieved although, clearly, after such a lapse of time, birds that are the equal of the old standard are not likely immediately to emerge, although very promising progress is being made.

POINTS OF THE SCOTCH FANCY

The Scotch Fancy canary is a member of a group of breeds that were called by the old-time fanciers "birds of position"; that is to say that they had a special type of posture in the show cage that was designed to show off their exhibition points to full advantage when in front of the judge.

Apart from "Glasgow Don", another old pet name of Scottish fanciers for their favourite was the "bird o'circle" which gives an indication of what that special posture was intended to be. From the tip of the beak to the end of the tail it was supposed to represent an almost unbroken arc of a circle, and the greater the curvature, the better specimen the bird was deemed to be.

To achieve such a position the bird should stand erect upon its perch, or even lean back a little. To balance this, the head should be carried well forward with the neck being extended and thus forming, along with the curved back and tail, a distinct convex curve. The underparts, consisting of the throat, breast and vent, should also be as nearly as possible hollowed out in the form of a curve, concave in this instance, so that the overall effect of the bird's shape would be something in the form of a half circle, or a crescent moon.

The greater the curvature, the more the bird was thought of and herein lay the reasons for the outcrossing with the Belgian that took place in the past. The latter breed had a notably long neck which was capable of being much extended and so the breeders of the Scotch Fancy hoped that, by introducing this feature into their birds, a still greater "reach" of the neck would be induced, thus encompassing a few more degrees of the desired circle.

This may well have been achieved but, unfortunately, at the expense of acquiring other Belgian characteristics as well, namely far too prominent shoulders, too straight a back and stiff and stilty legs — all of which are considered to be faults in the true Scotch Fancy.

The latter feature, in particular, was detrimental to another of the Scotch Fancy's show points, that which is known to fanciers as "travelling". At judging time, besides demonstrating its position, the bird is also required to show a lively action, moving freely from perch to perch, and for this supple legs are needed, stiff ones being a definite disadvantage.

These basic features of a well-circled crescent moon shape, plus freedom of movement, are attributes of the Scotch Fancy that should be regarded as the essential framework of the breed. The detailed points of its structure need somewhat closer examination.

The head should be on the small side, longish and somewhat flattened on the crown, giving to the bird something of a snaky appearance as in certain other breeds. It should never have any tendency to be at all rounded as in the Border or Fife canaries, for example.

The neck should be long, slender and tapering and capable of being well extended when the bird is in full pose, giving what has been previously referred to as "reach". A short, thick neck is the very opposite of this and should be avoided at all costs as, besides being incapable of much extension, it gives the bird a coarse look rather than the finely-drawn appearance that it should have.

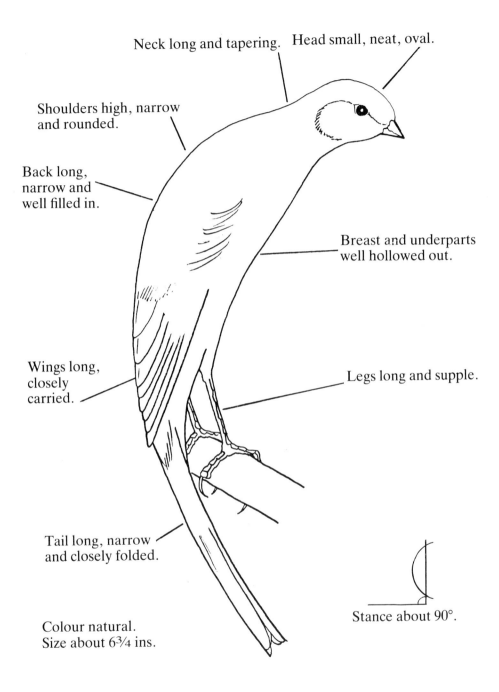

Neck long and tapering.

Head small, neat, oval.

Shoulders high, narrow and rounded.

Back long, narrow and well filled in.

Breast and underparts well hollowed out.

Wings long, closely carried.

Legs long and supple.

Tail long, narrow and closely folded.

Stance about 90°.

Colour natural.
Size about 6¾ ins.

21.1   The Points of a Scotch Fancy Canary

The shoulders should be high, narrow and nicely rounded, being well filled with feathers so that there is no depression between the wing butts. Yellows, being of less dense feather quality, sometimes tend to show this latter fault rather than do the buffs. The shoulders should not be prominent, as they are in the Belgian canary, although it must be appreciated that, when a good bird is in full posture showing plenty of reach, it cannot help but exhibit a certain amount of shoulder as well.

The back should be long, narrow and rounded. It should be well padded between the wings so that there is no suggestion of a "gutter" running down the middle and, of course, it should be well curved from the shoulder to the root of the tail to form a part of the whole circle of the bird. The wings should be of good length, fitting closely to the body and covering the rump. Drooping wings are considered to be a very bad fault.

The tail of the Scotch Fancy has always been an important feature because it plays an essential part in the balance of the bird. Unlike most other breeds, it must never be held firmly in line with the body but should be long and supple and swing freely well under the perch to complete as much curvature of outline as possible.

As previously described, the underside of the body should form the concave side of the crescent and so the breast should show no prominence but be well hollowed out. The whole of the under surface, from throat to tail, should then present a smooth and nicely tapered curve with no excess feathering at the waist.

The legs, as has already been indicated, are an important part of an exhibition specimen. Unless they are well set back, and are supple at the joint, the bird will have dificulty in taking up the correct position. If the legs are too straight it will tend to lean over the perch with the centre of gravity too far forward.

The Scotch Fancy should be a bird of fair size, by which **length** is indicated rather than bulk. The ideal bird, in fact, is on the slender side and the length as stated in the standard should be 6¾ inches although a little tolerance either way is permissible.

Feather quality has always been something of a problem and, at one period in the past, there was a good deal of support among breeders north of the border for a bird carrying quite a wealth of feather both on the shoulders and in the front as well. These failings tend to be inherited in some of today's specimens although improvement is taking place all the time.

Colour, as such, is of no material significance in the Scotch Fancy, as it is the shape and position of the bird that are the major considerations, and so the whole range of markings, both in buff and yellow are to be found as in other breeds of canary.

EXHIBITING THE SCOTCH FANCY

In a breed where position and freedom of movement are essential features of a show specimen, it follows that a fair amount of training may be necessary. At the same time, it is also true to say that in the very best specimens these attributes tend to be inherited and the bird seems to know instinctively what is required of it so that relatively little training may be needed.

As top class Scotch Fancies tend to be rather tense and "nervy" birds, great care must be exercised in their training for, if a bird becomes frightened of being in its show cage, or of having that cage handled, its whole show career could be ruined at the out-

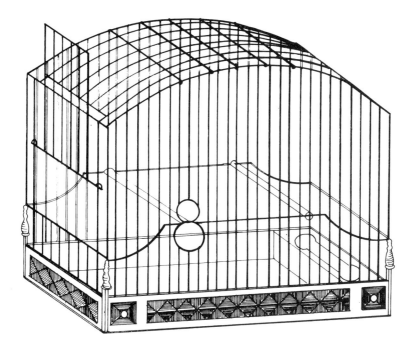

21.2   The Scotch Fancy Canary Show Cage

set. All of what has already been written on the subject of training is applicable to the Scotch Fancy, but perhaps to an even greater degree, with more care in handling, more attention to detail and more patience being needed so that the bird's progress is in no way rushed.

The end result, however, is well worth while when the bird will adopt its position with confidence, erect upon its perch with the head showing plenty of "drive" and the tail sweeping well beneath the perch. In action, too, with a mere indication from the judge's hand, it will move effortlessly from perch to perch displaying a certain jauntiness and elegance, yet without destroying the essential outline of its bodily contours.

The show cage for the Scotch Fancy is similar in general appearance to the more familiar Border Fancy cage (although the Scotch Fancy cage is, in fact, a much older insititution). The dimensions are somewhat larger to allow for the longer bird and for its "travelling" so that its tail swings clear and does not get caught up, either at the ends of the cage or between the perches which, in this cage must be a regulation six inches apart.

The measurements of the cage are 14 inches long, $9\frac{1}{2}$ inches high at each end rising to $11\frac{1}{2}$ inches high at the apex of the curve which forms the top. The depth from front to back is $4\frac{3}{4}$ inches, and there is a door at the left hand end and a drinker hole in the front opposite to the left hand perch. A seed drawer is provided at the bottom of the cage on the right.

In the past the wooden bases of these cages were beautifully made by craftsmen, often in mahogany and inlaid with other woods in geometrical designs, the whole being finished with a high gloss varnish or french polished. Some of these old cages have survived to the present-day and occasionally make their appearance upon the show bench, although more often they are treasured collector's items. In modern cages, a plain wooden base of any suitable wood may be used and should be varnished in a teak or mahogany finish.

At present, the classification for Scotch Fancies is fairly limited on account of their relatively low numbers.

OFFICIAL STANDARD

As was stated earlier in this chapter, the **Old Varieties Canary Assocation,** after consultation with all known breeders of the of the Scotch Fancy, decided that a return should be made to the original standard of a century ago. After slight rewording, to eliminate some ambiguity this was adopted in December, 1971. It is in the form of a Scale of Points covering the various features of the breed.

Scale of Points   *points*

Shape: Body long and tapering and curved in the form of a half circle, convex above, concave below, with a clean outline feather being close, short and tight.   20

Head and Neck: Small, neat, snaky head. Long, tapering neck.   10

Shoulders and Back: High, narrow, rounded shoulders, well filled in. Long, narrow, well-filled back, curving from shoulders to tail.   20

Tail: Long, narrow, closely folded and well curved under perch.   5

Style, Nerve and Travelling: Well raised up, forming a high circle. Bold, Free and jaunty carriage with plenty of life and action.   25

Size: Approximately 6¾ inches (17cm.).   10

Quality and Condition: Clean, healthy, perfect condition.   10

                                                                                                    ———

                                                                                        Total 100

                                                                                                    ———

Chapter 22

THE YORKSHIRE

HISTORY

The origins of the Yorkshire lay in a type of canary that was kept by the artisans in the woollen and mining communities of the county in the middle years of the last century. However, a great deal of outcrossing with other breeds was to take place in order to bring about desirable improvements in various directions so that the ultimate product can, perhaps, best be regarded as a "manufactured" variety. The great Victorian authors of books on canaries, who have frequently been alluded to in this present work, were there at the time to experience what was happening and so the facts have, fortunately, been well documented.

The first improvements took place by crossing the native Yorkshire canary with the neighbouring Lancashire in order to increase the size and overall length of the bird. This, not unexpectedly, was achieved at the expense of colour and feather quality and so the old-style Norwich was introduced to restore these qualities. Finally came the idea of imparting sleekness and elegance combined with a stylish show position, all of which were obtained from the (then) "king" of the canary fancy, the Belgian.

During this period of evolution, which took place mainly in the last quarter of the nineteenth century, it is little to be wondered at that the birds showed some considerable variation in type. However, with the foundation of the Yorkshire Canary Club in 1894, and agreement upon a definite standard, things rapidly began to improve.

This early standard of perfection called for a long, elegant and *very* slim bird; so slim, in fact, that the old time fanciers used to call it the "wedding ring" Yorkshire, meaning that it should be slim enough to pass through a wedding ring — an exaggeration, of course! Excellent progress followed and, during the first quarter of the present century, the Yorkshire rose to become one of the three foremost exhibition varieties in the country.

As explained in the chapter on "Standards and Specialist Societies", however, the ideas of breeders rarely remain static and, already by the late 1930's, there was appearing a Yorkshire of greater substance than before. This continued after the war until a bird with quite a substantial "top end" was finding favour with breeders and judges alike. This fact was recognised by the Southern Yorkshire Canary Club who were instrumental in adjusting the standard to accommodate the new type and in publishing an illustration of the ideal by S.R. Golding, both of which are here reproduced by permission.

Although these new trends have somewhat altered the outline of the original type of Yorkshire, many of the older virtues are still prized, namely a lengthy bird, an elegant and stylish posture, and excellent quality of feather.

POINTS OF THE YORKSHIRE

The Yorkshire is regarded by many connoisseurs as a supreme example of elegance and refinement in the canary world — a real tribute to the breeder's art — and it is certainly true that a good "Yorkie" wants a lot of beating. It is, perhaps, not the easiest of birds to bring to perfection for it is a large breed, of some considerable length, that must still possess the important attributes more often associated with the smaller ones, namely superb style and quality. These, coupled with its confident bearing and upright stance, have merited its one-time nickname of the "gentleman of the fancy".

It is, at the present time, the only widely kept variety of that group of breeds called by the old-time writers "birds of position" in which a sensitive and nervy action are combined with a graceful poise of the body as the bird displays itself in the show cage. This position is so important that one quarter of the total points allowed are for this feature alone, the desired attitude being erect and confident, with something of a swagger in its bearing. The Yorkshire should never stand across the perch at a low angle nor show any inclination to crouch, either of which will ruin the bird's chances on the show bench. The legs are long, straight and strong and yet quite supple with none of the stiltiness seen, for example, in the Belgian.

Of equal value on the points scale is the characteristic recognised by every knowledgeable fancier as the hall-mark of quality, namely fine, close and "boxy" feathering. No suspicion of coarseness in the way of eyebrows, looseness at the thighs, or a frill at the breast should be seen. The wings, although long, should be tightly carried close to the body with the tips of the primaries and secondaries in a neat line and meeting evenly down the centre of the back. The long tail, too, must be tightly folded, never being wide and spreading or what is called "fish-tailed", a blemish that would spoil the balanced appearance of a good Yorkshire.

These essential characteristics of carriage and feather quality in no way differ from the earlier standard but it is in the type, or conformation of the body, that the greatest changes are to be seen in the modern Yorkshire. Although it is still essentially a long and stylish-looking bird, it no longer has the ultra slim figure of earlier days, possessing now, in particular, a proportionately larger head, neck and shoulders in relation to the rest of the body.

The head, instead of small and round, is now described in the standard as being "full". It is quite broad and long, with the back of the skull appearing to come well down towards the shoulders with but little indication of the presence of the neck. The shoulders also are broad and well rounded and the back is well filled with no suggestion of a depression running down the centre. In side view, after the rise of the shoulders, it is quite straight as far as the root of the tail.

The underside, starting just below the beak, again shows little suggestion of any neck but is nicely rounded with a deep chest which then tapers gradually away cleanly between the legs towards the vent and base of the tail. Along with the line of the back, this then gives a long finely drawn out taper to the body which, as stated before, must not be hidden in excessive feather at the waist, thighs or vent. The tail of the Yorkshire differs from that of most other breeds of canary in that, instead of being carried in an exact prolongation of the line of the body, it should have a just perceptible "lift" to it, but not so pronounced as to make the bird robin-tailed.

140

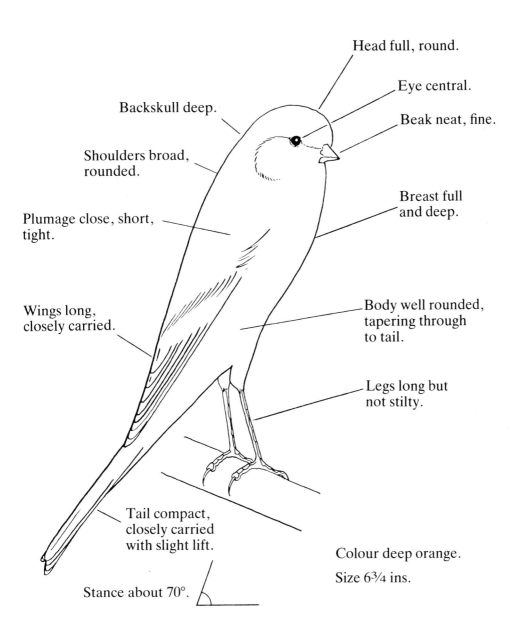

Head full, round.

Eye central.

Beak neat, fine.

Backskull deep.

Shoulders broad, rounded.

Breast full and deep.

Plumage close, short, tight.

Body well rounded, tapering through to tail.

Wings long, closely carried.

Legs long but not stilty.

Tail compact, closely carried with slight lift.

Colour deep orange.

Size 6¾ ins.

Stance about 70°.

22.1   The Points of a Yorkshire Canary

The Yorkshire is one of the larger breeds of canary, the standard quoting 6¾ inches as an approximate length, although many first class exhibition birds may well exceed this figure.

EXHIBITING THE YORKSHIRE

Like all other breeds that are required to show a position in the show cage, rather than any movement, the Yorkshire is exhibited in a show cage that has only one perch (apart from those provided for access to the drinker and seed trough) upon which it should stand, alert and upright, in a guardsman-like attitude. This cage is of an open wire pattern with a wooden base, but differs from those of the Belgian, Lancashire, Frills, etc. in having an arched top instead of a flat one. The specifications are rigidly laid down (as in all show cages) so as to ensure complete uniformity and give no bird any unfair advantage. The details are as follows:

> Length 9¼ inches overall, with 17 wires. Width 6¼ inches overall with 12 wires. Height 14 inches overall. Base 3⅛ inches deep (from ¼ inch wood).
> Seed Trough ¾ inch wide inside, and 1 inch deep outside, the top edge of the Seed Hopper to be rounded and to be ¼ inch below the top edge of the base. Cages to have 3mm. Plywood base. First Crossbar 6⅜ inches from base, second crossbar 10¼ inches high from base. Corner wires and cross wires to be 14 s.w.g., the other wires 17 s.w.g.
> Cages to be fitted with three ⅝ x ⅜ inch white oval perches, the two bottom perches shall be fixed on the fourth wire from either end of the cage, the top perch to be fixed on the ninth wire from either end of the cage. The perches must be fixed in the cage with the curved side uppermost. All cages to be finished Black all over.
> The Water Hole to be large enough to allow the bird easy access to the water.

Show cage training for the Yorkshire follows the same pattern as that for all other birds of position and these were fully detailed in the chapter on the Belgian canary. Of the more popular breeds, probably none requires greater attention in the matter of training, nor responds better to it, than does the Yorkshire and the exhibitor who is prepared to spend plenty of time on his charges will be well repaid.

The classification of Yorkshire canaries differs somewhat from that of most other breeds being based upon a slightly different interpretation of some definitions. It is essential, therefore, that the exhibitor is conversant with these when showing under the rules of a Yorkshire specialist society. These are given after the official standard of the breed. All of the usual range of colours are to be encountered, both in green and cinnamon, and whites also are often seen. The yellow ground birds are colour fed for exhibition purposes and, although they rarely possess quite so deep a tone as the Norwich, it is important that it should be as pure and level as possible throughout the body.

OFFICIAL STANDARD

The following standard and scale of points is agreed to by all Yorkshire specialist societies:

22.2   Yorkshire Canary Show Cage

22.3   Official Standard Portrait of the Yorkshire Canary
Issued by the Southern Yorkshire Canary Club

THE YORKSHIRE

SCALE OF POINTS

points

Head — Full, round and cleanly defined. Backskull deep and carried back in line with rise of shoulders. Eye as near centre of head as possible. Shoulders proportionately broad, rounded and carried well up to and gradually merging into head. Breast full and deep, corresponding to width and rise of shoulders and carried up full to base of beak which should be neat and fine. 20

Body — Well rounded and gradually tapering throughout to tail. 10

Position — Attitude erect with fearless carriage, legs long without being stilty, and slight lift behind. 25

Feather — Close, short and tight. Wings proportionately long and evenly carried down the centre of the back and firmly set on a compact and closely folded tail. 25

Size — Length approximately 6¾ inches with corresponding symmetrical proportions. 10

Condition — Health, cleanliness and sound feather, colour pure and level. 10

_____

100

_____

STANDARD OF MARKINGS

The presence of dark feather on the thighs or natural discolouration of the beak, legs or feet or any mark that is not discernible as the bird stands in its natural position in the show cage, shall be entirely ignored throughout the whole classification.

Ticked — A ticked bird shall have one mark only unbroken by any intervening light feather on any part of the body (thighs, legs, feet and beak excluded).

The standards for Marked Birds shall be regulated by what are termed technical marks, that is marks on (touching) eyes, flights (primary or/and secondary) and sides of tail. Each eye mark and each tail mark must be distinctly separated from its corresponding mark by a portion of light feathers. A bird which has a cap, or grizzle, which touches both eyes is for the purpose of our classification considered to have one technical mark only. A bird with a tail consisting of all dark feathers is for the purpose of our classification considered to have one Technical Mark only as there are no intervening light feathers.

Evenly Marked — An evenly marked bird shall have —
(a) Two technical marks (both eyes, or flights of both wings, or both sides of tail), or
(b) Four technical marks (both eyes and flights of both wings, or both eyes and both sides of tail, or flights of both wings and both sides of tail), or
(c) All six technical marks.

Unevenly Marked — An unevenly marked bird shall have three or five technical marks only.

Variegated Classes — Shall consist of any other variegation not already provided.
(a) Lightly variegated, more light than dark.
(b) Heavily variegated, more dark than light.

145

A "Self" Bird is All Dark.

A "Foul" Bird has light feathers in wing flights or tail **only.** The presence of light feathers apart from wing flights or/and tail make it a variegated bird.

A number of Yorkshire canary specialist societies exist in various parts of Great Britain, most of them welcoming members from any part of the country.

APPENDIX

GLOSSARY

For ready reference, a glossary of terms and definitions commonly used by exhibitors is given below. Most of these are dealt with more fully in the chapters on the breeds to which they refer.

Action — Refers to the general agility of the bird. Particularly applied to such breeds as the Border and Scotch Fancy.

Agate — In coloured canaries, the dilute green mutation. May be present as gold agate, red agate, silver agate, rose agate, etc.

Bald Face — A serious blemish in the Lizard canary in which the cap encroaches upon the face and cheeks of the bird.

Bloom — The high sheen or polish that appears on the plumage of birds that are in perfect health and condition.

Blue — The "self-green" form of the *white* canary. Generally of a slate blue colour.

Broken Capped — A category in the Lizard canary in which the bird's light cap is broken to a greater or lesser extent by dark feathering.

Browy — Possessing long feathering over the eyes. A desirable point in breeds such as the Crest and Lancashire, but objectionable in most others.

Buff — One of the two major feather types in the canary. The lipochrome pigment stops just short of the margin of the web of the feather giving the bird a lightly powdered or frosted appearance.

"C" — Means Commended; an old time "courtesy" award equalling seventh in class.

Cap — In the Lizard canary, the light area of feathering on the crown of the head.

Cap Marked — A *dark* area of feathers on the top of the head in other canaries.

Carriage — The general stance of the bird. May vary from breed to breed, being upright, semi-upright or at a low-angle. Whichever it is the bird should still be smart and stylish, never slovenly.

Champion — The senior status achieved by an exhibitor after winning three first prizes in Novice classes in Open competition, usually with a minimum qualifying number of exhibits and/or a period of time.

Cinnamon — A very early mutation in the canary in which the black melanin pigment is absent, leaving only the brown. In coloured canary circles they now use the word brown, e.g. a red orange *brown* is a red orange cinnamon.

Classification — The system by which canaries are divided into various categories for the purpose of exhibition.

Clear — A bird possessing no dark pigmentation in its plumage at all. Usually, any dark marks on beak, legs or feet are disregarded, also any dark underflue so long as it does not show on the surface as the bird stands on its perch.

Clear Capped — A Lizard canary whose cap is unbroken by an dark feathering, provided that it has a reasonably regular outline.

Cobby — Short and stocky in build. A desirable feature in some breeds, especially the Norwich.

Colour Fed — Given special food at moulting time to turn the plumage to some shade of orange. Used by breeders of Lizards, Norwich, Red Factors and Yorkshires, but not by others.

Condition — The general high state of health and cleanliness in which a bird should be shown. Most standards allocate a specific number of points for this.

Consort — The plainhead bird of the Gloster Fancy breed.

Coppy — the crested bird of the Lancashire breed. Also often used for the crest itself.

Corona — The crested bird of the Gloster Fancy breed.

Crest — Either the general term used for this particular feature in any breed, or specifically as a shortened form for the Crested canary.

Dimorphic — In coloured canary circles, a mutant form in which the colour is confined to four small areas only, namely the face, shoulders, rump and breast.

Dominant White — One of two mutations that have produced white canaries. Nearly all whites found in the type breeds are of the dominant kind. (Note — A competent textbook on canaries should explain the mode of inheritance and the technique of breeding whites of either mutation).

Drinkers — In general, any vessels for holding the bird's water. Show cage drinkers are of specified patterns which may vary from breed to breed.

Drive — Used by Scotch Fancy breeders to describe the desirable forward thrust of the head to give the bird as much "reach" as possible.

Even Marked — A bird whose markings are evenly balanced on either side of the body. See Technical Markings for details.

Eye Marked — A bird with a dark mark touching one or both eyes.

Fancy — Epithet attached to the names of several breeds, e.g. Border Fancy, Gloster Fancy, Scotch Fancy, etc. It denotes a breed that has been developed for particular points of beauty, based upon arbitrary characteristics that have been agreed upon by fanciers.

Feather Quality — Describes the form and texture of the body feathering which, in most breeds, should be close, short and tight, with a fine bloom or sheen to it.

Fins — Of Frilled canaries, bunches of feathers starting from just above the thighs and sweeping outwards and upwards around the wings.

Flights — The main flying feathers of the wings, divided into the primaries (the longer ones) and the secondaries (the shorter ones). In all breeds they should be tightly folded and carried close to the body, with the tips just meeting in a neat line.

Flue — The soft fluffy part of the feather next to the bird's skin. Does not normally show itself on the surface.

Foul — An otherwise dark, self coloured bird that may have some white feathers (usually not more than three in number) in the wings or tail.

Foul Tail — A tail as described above.

Foul Wing — A wing as described above. Both of these are serious faults in the Lizard canary.

Frills, Frilling — The curled feathers that characterises all of the Frilled breeds. A serious fault in most other varieties.

Frontal — The forward part of a crest, flowing over the beak.

Gold — In the Lizard, the yellow bird as opposed to the buff (silver). In coloured canaries, all yellow ground birds whether yellow or buff.

Green — A bird possessing the original wild type of plumage, unbroken by any light feathering.

Grizzled — An admixture of minute light and dark specks forming a greyish mark instead of the normal dark (green) mark. Often found in the crests of Crested, Gloster or Lancashire canaries.

Ground Colour — The basic lipochrome colour of a feather ignoring any melanins that may be present. It may be yellow, white, red or rose.

"H.C." — Means Highly Commended. An old award equivalent to sixth in the class.

Heavily Variegated — A bird in which more than half of its plumage has dark pigmentation.

Horned — A bad fault in all crested breeds in which some feathers are out of place in the form of small tufts resembling horns.

Ino — A fairly recent mutation in the coloured canary characterised, among other things, by having red eyes.

Isabel — In coloured canaries, the dilute cinnamon mutation. May be present as Gold Isabel, Silver Isabel, etc.

Ivory — Another mutant form in coloured canaries consisting of a dilution of the yellow lipochrome to a smooth ivory shade. Sometimes also known as the lipochrome pastel.

Jabot — In Frilled canaries, the frills on the breast curling forwards and upwards under the chin to form a kind of frilly shirt front.

Jonque — The yellow bird of the now extinct London Fancy canary.

Lacing — Of the Lizard; the fine margin of lighter colour around the edges of the wing covert feathers.

Lightly Variegated — A bird in which less than half of its plumage has dark pigmentation.

Mantle — Of frilled canaries; formed by the feathers of the back which are divided by a long, straight, central parting and fall forwards over the bird's shoulders like a cage.

Marked — A bird which may have dark feathering on (touching) the eyes, the secondary flights or outer tail feathers. (See Technical Markings).

Mealy — Used to describe the frosting of buff canaries. *Over* mealiness is a fault in most breeds.

Members Show — A show at which entry is confined to members of the promoting society only.

Melanins — The dark pigments found in the canary's plumage, consisting of black (eumelanin) and brown (phaeomelanin).

Non Capped — A Lizard canary that has no cap at all, the feathers of the head being covered by the normal spangled type as found in the rest of the body.

Non Frosted — Used in coloured canary circles to denote birds of the "yellow" feather type — the word yellow being considered somewhat inappropriate when the bird may actually be red or pink!

Novice — The category in which every newcomer to the canary fancy is entitled to exhibit until he qualifies as a Champion. Minor details may differ from club to club, but a generally accepted definition is; an exhibitor who, at the commencement of the show season, has not yet won three first prizes in Open competition as a Novice. There is usually a minimum qualifying number of exhibitors required, also a minium number of staged exhibits. Some clubs grant the Novice a certain number of years irrespective of how many wins are achieved.

Opal — A mutation in the coloured canary involving dilution of the melanin pigments, pencilling being of a silvery grey colour.

Open Show — A show at which entry is open to all comers and not restricted to members of the promoting society.

Over Capped — A serious fault in Lizard canaries in which the cap runs down into the neck.

Overshown — A bird that has become jaded and lacking in lustre due to having been shown too frequently.

Pencilling — The dark markings in the forms of streaks that are seen in the canary's plumage on back and flanks. They are black in greens and brown in cinnamons and, in general, should be clearly visible but not too heavy.

Pink Eyed — A characteristic of cinnamon birds, clearly visible only when nestlings. As the bird becomes older the iris turns so dark a brown as to be difficult to distinguish.

Plainhead — A bird without any crest to its head. Usually only applied in the Lancashire breed, although the Norwich is still widely referred to as the Norwich Plainhead — a hangover from the days when it needed to be distinguished from the Crested Norwich.

Position — The charactertistic posture of a bird which should always be typical of its particular breed.

Racy — The opposite of "cobby", i.e. slim and finely drawn. Not to be admired in any breed except, perhaps, Belgians and Scotch Fancies.

Recessive White — Another mutation that gave rise to white canaries. The mode of inheritance is quite different from that of the Dominant White (which see).

Reach — Of the Scotch Fancy. A desirable feature in which the bird stretches out its long neck as far as possible.

Rolls — Applied to several song passages of the Roller canary in which the tempo of the beats is so fast as to make them almost inseparable to the human ear.

Rose — The lipochrome pastel mutation in Red canaries which has produced a ground colour of a bright, deep, rich pink. (c.f. Ivory in yellow ground birds).

Rowing — Of the Lizard; the markings on the bird's breast and flanks formed in a similar manner to the spangling on the back.

Satinette — Another fairly recent mutation in coloured canaries which, like the ino, has red eyes.

Self — A bird possessing feathering that is completely solid in melanin pigment and unbroken by any light feathers anywhere in body, wings or tail.

Schedule — A document (usually a small booklet) sent out by show promoting societies in which are given full details of date, location, rules, classification, prizes, etc. appertaining to their show. Also contains an *Entry Form* upon which the intending exhibitor must make his entries.

Silver — In Lizard canaries, the buff feather type (c.f. gold). In coloured canaries, birds with a *white* ground colour, e.g. Silver Agate, Silver Opal, etc.

Slipped Claw — A crippled condition of the foot in which (usually) the hind claw is dislocated, either by slipping forwards under the other three, or backwards against the shank (here, often referred to as stiff hind claw). A bird suffering from this disability should never be shown as it cannot grip the perch and stand properly.

Snaky — An exceptionally sleek and almost reptilian shape to the head, desirable in the Belgian, Gibber Italicus and Scotch Fancy but a fault in most other breeds.

Soft — Means Soft Condition, i.e. a bird out of condition, being often loose in feather, dull of eye and with little vitality.

Spangling — The essential feature of Lizard canaries, which is formed by a series of perfectly straight and parallel rows of black crescent shaped spots running down the back of the bird and standing out distinctly from the ground colour.

Split Crest — A crest in which the ideal circular shape is spoiled by gaps showing in it.

Standard — The criterion by which any breed is judged, representing the degree of excellence to which the breeder should aspire.

Technical Markings — Dark feathers on an otherwise clear bodied bird that are confined to three points only, namely the eyes, the secondary feathers and the outer tail feathers. According to how many of these marks it possesses, a bird may be two, four or six pointed (evenly marked), or three or five pointed (unevenly marked). Not many breed societies nowadays make specific use of these definitions in their classification.

Three Parts Dark — A bird possessing not less than 75% dark feathering.

Ticked — A bird possessing a *single* dark mark anywhere on the body that is coverable by a 1p piece, OR having no more than three adjacent dark feathers in wing or tail which thus also form a *single* dark mark.

Toenails — Should always be kept trim and neat except in the case of Parisian Frills whose nails should be long and curly like a corkscrew. Missing toenails are a physical defect not likely to be overlooked by a judge.

Tours — Various song passages of the Roller canary delivered at a slower tempo than the rolls, and in which the individual "beats" can be clearly distinguished.

Type — The sum total of the basic features that together characterise any particular breed and distinguish it from all others.

Variety — A word freely used by fanciers as interchangeable with "breed" but strictly speaking it should not be. A variety is a subdivision within a breed which differs in some recognisable way from the remainder of its kind, e.g. the Cinnamon Norwich is a *variety* of the Norwich canary, the Green Border is a *variety* of the Border Fancy, etc.

"V.H.C." — Means Very Higly Commended. another old time award equivalent to fifth in class.

Work — Applied by breeders of Lizard canaries to the excellence (or otherwise) of the markings in their variety, especially those on the breast and flanks. (e.g. "full of work", "lacks work", etc).

"W.C." — Means Wrong Class. If a bird has been wrongly entered, the judge will write "W.C." on the cage label, usually adding the reason for his rejection of the exhibit.

Yellow — The other basic type in canaries in which the lipochrome pigment extends all over the web of the feather right to the very edges. (c.f. buff).

Young Stock Show — A show held, usually as a members only show, in which young birds prior to their first moult can be exhibited. Classes are often put on for adult birds as well so that the show will be reasonably well supported.

Plate 23

Padovan Frilled Canary

Plate 24

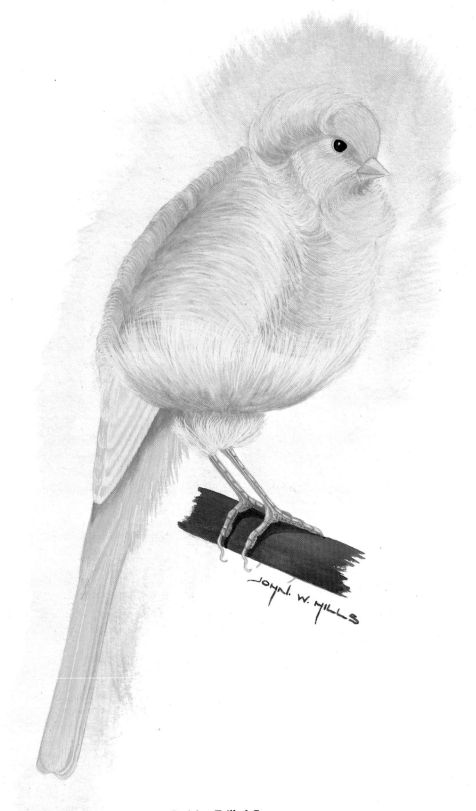

Parisian Frilled Canary